The Mirror of Criticism

By the same author

FICTION

The Inventory
Words
The Present
Mobius the Stripper (Stories and Short Plays)
Four Stories
Migrations
The Echo Chamber
Vergil Dying
The Air We Breathe

NON-FICTION

The World and the Book
The Lessons of Modernism
The Modern English Novel (ed)
The Siren's Song: Selected Essays by Maurice Blanchot (ed)
Writing and the Body

The Mirror of Criticism

Selected Reviews, 1977-1982

GABRIEL JOSIPOVICI
Reader in English, University of Sussex

THE HARVESTER PRESS · SUSSEX
BARNES & NOBLE BOOKS · NEW JERSEY

First published in Great Britain in 1983 by
THE HARVESTER PRESS LIMITED
Publisher: John Spiers
16 Ship Street, Brighton, Sussex
and in the USA by
BARNES & NOBLE BOOKS
81 Adams Drive, Totowa, New Jersey 07512

© Gabriel Josipovici, 1983

British Library Cataloguing in Publication Data

    Josipovici, Gabriel
        The mirror of criticism.
        1. Criticism
        I. Title
        801'.95   PN81

        ISBN 0-7108-0499-7

Library of Congress Cataloging in Publication Data

Josipovici, Gabriel, 1940-
  The mirror of criticism.

    1. Literature — History and criticism —
Addresses, essays, lectures. I. Title.
PN710.J67   1983   809   83-2814
ISBN 0-389-20388-2

Photoset in 10 on 11 point Baskerville by
Alacrity Phototypesetters, Banwell Castle, Weston-super-Mare.
Printed in Great Britain by
Biddles Ltd, Guildford, Surrey

All rights reserved

*To Stephen Medcalf and Tony Nuttall,
good walkers, good readers*

Contents

1	Introduction	1
2	True Mastery	13
3	What Was Chaucer Really Up To?	23
4	Reading the Middle Ages	38
5	A Great Critic	47
6	Rabelais and the Role of Fiction	54
7	A Life and a Half	66
8	Three Thousand Years of Poetry	72
9	The Last Great Book	81
10	Life and Letters	84
11	Saneness and Wisdom	88
12	Radiance and Interpretation	93
13	A Ghost in the City	99
14	A Childish Vision	102
15	A Happy Man	106
16	A Sense of Waste	108
17	The Heart of the Matter	118
18	Body and Mind	128
19	The Ethics of Silence	136
20	A Modern Poet	141
21	On the Brink of Parable	145
22	A Triumphant Return	150
23	The Really Real	153
24	The Demythologising Imagination	157
25	The Hand and the Eye	162
26	Conclusion: From the Other Side of the Fence, or True Confessions of an Experimentalist	173
	ACKNOWLEDGEMENTS	181

1
Introduction

Why is the profoundest criticism to be found in the letters and incidental remarks of artists?

I am not thinking here only of the famous letters of Keats on Shakespeare or Coleridge on Wordsworth, which show evidence of long and loving acquaintance, but even of such passing remarks as Kafka's on Gerhard Hauptmann's *Anna* ('I recognise the master's touch in the structure, in the wit and animated dialogue, in many passages, but the whole thing is such a bag of wind!'), or Wallace Stevens' on Hans Arp ('The human spirit has nothing to fear from him.').

Critical pronouncements of this kind, in a letter or a journal, have the advantage that they do not need to be substantiated. The writer gives voice to his feelings and then moves on to something else. He feels no inhibition about showing doubt or uncertainty, leaving off abruptly, changing his mind in mid-sentence and doing all those other natural things which the critical book or essay has somehow to pretend we are not subject to. Yet if this were all we might be inclined to wonder if this was indeed a gain. For it could be argued that true criticism is precisely that which has come to terms with hesitation and doubt, has thought through the implications of certain responses, and is, for that very reason, a deeper and a richer thing than a passing comment in a letter or a journal.

There is some truth in this. But it may be that the losses involved in the transition from immediate response to considered judgement outweigh the gains. For what the letter conveys, and what the book or essay, however sensitively written, conceals, is the sense of an *encounter*. Keats' remarks, in the letter to his brothers about negative capability, tell us something about Keats and something about Shakespeare, but, more important, they convey to us dramatically the significance for

Keats of his encounter with Shakespeare. When Coleridge writes that he finds himself disturbed by 'a daring humbleness of language and versification, and a strict adherence to matter of fact, even to prolixity', in certain poems of Wordsworth's, the fact that these things disturb him cannot be disentangled from the rest of his remarks. What is important is not that Wordsworth's poems are being described in one way or another, but that their 'daring humbleness' has had a peculiar and violent effect on one particularly responsive reader.

The remarks of Keats and Coleridge are not aesthetic comments. Or rather, their significance lies in the fact that they make us aware that aesthetics cannot be hived off from the rest of life. Similarly, Hauptmann's rustic epic confirms Kafka in his feelings that the well-written work, however well it is written, holds no interest for him. It makes him realise once more (the remark comes in a letter written towards the end of his life) that for him the real question has never been: How can I write as well as this? but: Why should I write this kind of thing at all? And, if not this, then what? The encounter with Arp's work reveals to Stevens, through what it lacks, that the greatest art is an affront as well as a pleasure; that there is an art which is good, intelligent, aesthetically pleasing, but which we will never feel to be really important because it never quite dares to be more than that, to recognise its dangerous power. Of course Stevens is not equating such recognition with the naïve aggression of certain forms of *avant-garde* theatre, but rather with the self.contained and luminous works of Plato, Dante and Shakespeare. But also, of course, with his own secret aims and ambitions. For what we are made aware of in these moments of encounter is the hidden project of the artist revealing itself (to him as much as to us) as it comes into contact with another project, one which has already been realised.

Now a project, the shape we give our lives, partly consciously and partly unconsciously, naturally involves choices, sacrifices, losses as well as gains. Indeed, there can be no gain without some kind of renunciation. And this is what a critical comment in an artist's letter conveys to us. It is never neutral, never the simple registering of the acquisition of knowledge, but rather the startled recognition of needs and choices. 'You admire, I love!' Stravinsky said bitterly when accused of distorting Pergolesi for his own ends in *Pulcinella*, and though the critic might be tempted to treat this as a typical artist's defence, in other words no defence at all, it is Stravinsky who is the better critic. For 'I love' means that I am prepared to give up

INTRODUCTION

something for something else; admiration costs nothing at all.

The most wonderful literary expression of an encounter of the kind I have been describing is to be found in Dante's *Commedia*. In the first meeting of Dante and Virgil, as in the later meeting of the two pilgrims with Statius, we are made to realise that encounter here has meant nothing less than conversion. 'Or se' tu quel Virgilio e quella fonte / che spandi di parlar si largo fiume?' ['Are you then that Virgil, that fount which pours forth so broad a stream of speech?'] asks Dante, and the image, as always in this poem, is chosen with care. For Virgil is to play in this story the role of John the Baptist to Beatrice's Jesus, and his 'stream of speech' is nothing less than a new Jordan in which the poet will be baptised. Virgil's is the voice crying in the wilderness, in that 'gran diserto' where the two poets first meet, and which is also the desert of Dante's own life prior to that encounter.

Of course not all encounters are of quite this kind; nor does all criticism to be found in the letters of artists rise to this peak of intensity. What I am trying to suggest, however, is that even the very best 'straight' criticism, by the very fact that it is to be found in books and articles which seem somehow to exist by themselves, to be there, regardless of the life and choices of the critic, has the effect of making us forget that our response to art is never purely neutral, never merely aesthetic, that if we respond fully we must recognise that it is our whole mental landscape which has been changed, if ever so slightly, by this or that work.

I am not reiterating the old charge that criticism is arid, that it is somehow cut off from life. I am suggesting rather that there is something inherent in the act of criticism itself which makes it fail *even on its own terms*; makes it fail, that is, fully to explicate and illuminate works of art.

Let me give two examples of criticism in operation, to contrast with the extracts from the writers' letters quoted above. Gerard Genette is one of the subtlest and most intelligent critics now writing. His extended essay on narrative, *Discours du récit*, which is also an essay on Proust's great novel, is one of the finest pieces of criticism to have appeared since the war. To read it is not only to be made to understand Proust better, but to find that one has been given the tools to respond to a whole range of narratives with deeper understanding. One of Genette's most important contributions is his exploration of what he calls the 'iterative' mode in Proust. By this he means that Proust, unlike most novelists, gives us a sense not so much of a plot unfolding as of the multiple repetitions which make up daily life. Proust's manner of proceeding is not to say: 'One day', or 'That Saturday', but 'Saturdays at Combray', or 'In the spring' we did such and such. In Genette's words: 'The text of *Combray* tells us, in the imperfect of repetition, not what *has passed*, but what *used to pass* at Combray, regularly, ritually, every day, or every Sunday, or every Saturday, etc.' (Genette's qualities as a critic depend not only on the clarity of his thought but also on the precision and elegance of his language. How he actually puts it, untranslatably, is 'non ce qui *s'est passé*, mais ce qui *se passait* a Combray...') Of course, Proust manages to have it both ways: to present us with unique events, such as the scene in which Marcel is able to persuade his mother to stay the night with him, *and* to maintain the sense of the daily, the monthly, the yearly routine. Genette's analysis, and his introduction of the term 'iterative', are extremely helpful; once we have focused on what it is Proust does we can better appreciate the effect his novel has on us, an effect of density, or saturation, missing from even the greatest novels of the nineteenth century.

Yet the introduction of this useful term, at the same time as it illuminates, also obscures. For iteration in Proust is not just a technique, or even a mode of vision, it is also a *problem*. On the one hand repetition is beneficial, it is the daily expectation of joy in childhood, it is that which makes the recapturing of those childhood days possible, and it is even that which makes it possible for Marcel to grasp the nature of his vocation, for what else are the experiences of the *madeleine* and the uneven paving-stones if not further examples of repetition? But iteration has another aspect: it is that compulsive repetition which, Marcel comes to discover, is the central law of love and perhaps of life itself: we think we are moving forward into a new life and find it is only the old one, with all its frustrations and inadequacies, in a new guise.

Now the interesting thing is that Genette's very precision in isolating the iterative as the dominant mode in Proust is in a way responsible for his inability to explore and explain its link with frustration and loss. Our ability to stand above the detail of the narrative and grasp what it is up to, an ability much enhanced by the use of the tool which is the term 'iterative', is precisely what stops us experiencing the negative side of repetition. Yet this is certainly something we experience when we read the book; but we seem to be able to experience it only *by* reading the book, by investing time and emotion and imagination in

INTRODUCTION

entering Marcel's world. Only because that time, our time, has been so invested, can we also experience its frustration. But criticism, by its very nature, its explicative function, frees us from compulsion and confusion. The tendency of criticism is thus always towards idealisation; it always tends to view art as a triumph.

But the triumph of art can also lie in its ability to articulate failure and frustration and loss, and thus to render these bearable. The triumph of art, in Proust, as in Kafka and Virginia Woolf, lies precisely in its refusal to accept easily the comforts of the imagination, and therefore of art itself.

But lest it be thought that this kind of vision is confined to modern literature, let me give another example, this time of a type of criticism which is imaginatively allied not to linguistics but to historical scholarship. Herbert wrote many striking poems and many striking couplets; two of the most famous are to be found in 'The Sacrifice' and 'The Agonie':

> Man stole the fruit, but I must climbe the tree;
> The tree of life to all but onely me...

and:

> Love is that liquor sweet and most divine
> Which my God feels as bloud; but I as wine.

I have no wish to reactivate the arguments which raged over both couplets in academic circles in the 1940s and 1950s. It seems to me evident that it is important for both passages to know something about Christian theology and ritual. In the first Herbert is wittily using the central notion of *figura*, that way of looking at history inaugurated by the Gospels and Pauline epistles, which saw Jesus as a second Adam, the Cross as a second Edenic tree, the Jordan as a second Red Sea, the twelve apostles as prefigured in the twelve tribes, and so on. The point to this system of correspondences was not the desire for symmetry but the wish to prove that God looks down the corridor of history, so to speak, and has prefigured the Incarnation in the actual events of history as they are recounted in the Hebrew scriptures. Though historians of theology and art had long been aware of this tradition, literary scholars cottoned on to it rather late in the day. Erich Auerbach, Rosemond Tuve and Northrop Frye (in the wake perhaps of Mann's *Joseph and His Brethren*) more than made up for lost time though, and, in their use of *figura* to illuminate earlier literature, quite transformed literary studies. And yet here too we come upon a sort of paradox connected with understanding and non-understanding. For the scholarship which revealed the figural basis to Herbert's work, and the criticism which made the further point that Herbert was using the tradition in a uniquely compressed and witty way, also, inadvertently, deflected our response to the poems. For, no less than Marcel in Proust's novel, Jesus only makes the connections between Old and New Testaments, asserts *figura*, at a cost. '... but I must climbe the tree' carries with it a temporal dimension of pain, effort and doubt which our substitution of the word *figura*, or of the liturgical connotations of the image, tends to obliterate.

For the liturgy too is a problem, and not an explanation. Church services, just like poems, are to be lived through, and cannot simply be understood. This is made very clear in the second couplet. When we actually read the poem we are made to struggle with 'which my God feels as bloud; but I as wine'; and to explain that in the Eucharist the one is transformed into the other is to remove the tension between pain and triumph which the poem holds so delicately in the balance. Yet even talk of tension or ambiguity will not help one — there seems to be an unbridgeable gap between our response to the poem and anything criticism can do or say.

Genette, to give him his due, is only too aware of this. 'The semiotic universe', he ends by saying, 'has a horror of the void, and to *name* contingency is already to assign to it a function, to impose a meaning upon it. Even — and especially — when it is silent, criticism always says too much. The best thing would perhaps be, like the Proustian narrative itself, never to "finish", that is, in a sense, never to start.' The trouble with this, as with Northrop Frye's rather similar remark that since the actual experience of reading is private and incommunicable, we should concentrate on those aspects of literature which *can* be talked about, is that it remains a gesture. It does not remove the problem, it merely shelves it. The problem stays with us: the need to speak our experience of the art that moves us, and the recognition that to speak it is in some way to annul or distort it.

Herbert's resolutions, tentative though they are, tend to be couched in terms of the renewal of the possibility of prayer, of dialogue, or in quasi-biological terms of growth, or in both together, as in the second and last stanza of his poem, 'The News':

> Oh that my prayers! mine, alas!
> Oh that some Angel might a trumpet sound;

INTRODUCTION

> At which the Church falling upon her face
> Should crie so loud, untill the trump were drown'd,
> That your sweet sap might come again!

Criticism, by its very nature, denies that 'Oh' and that 'sap', just as it cannot hold together the profound contradictions Proust discovers in the nature of time. It cannot help denying because it comes *after* the event; it is safe, but its safety is also the sign of its exclusion.

It was an awareness, of course, of the contradictions lying at the heart of the notion of explanation which fuelled the work of two of the nineteenth century's greatest critics, Nietzsche and Kierkegaard. (I am being deliberately ambiguous: they were the greatest literary critics because they were so critical of their age.) Both realised that it is not that certain things cannot be talked about, but that to talk about them inevitably transforms them into something else. In *Fear and Trembling*, Kierkegaard's whole effort is directed to making us understand how much of a betrayal of Abraham is our assumption that we can understand his state of mind as he prepares to sacrifice Isaac. Kierkegaard sets up a whole series of parallels and then shows that none is a real parallel; he gives a variety of explanations, but only in order to convey to us that none can be the real explanation. Not only that. The whole work is presented not as Kierkegaard's own meditation but as that of a pseudonymous author. Yet despite all these twistings and turnings we sense in Kierkegaard, as we do in Nietzsche's later work, a growing despair at the realisation that what is most in need of speech cannot be spoken, that there is a built-in contradiction to their whole enterprise, since if we are persuaded by them and say: 'Ah, so I don't understand!' then we have not understood; but if we do understand — or think we do — then they have also failed.

More recent critics who start from the same set of insights, such as Derrida, have perhaps been less aware of the difficulties of what they are trying to do. They keep writing philosophy and criticism which insists more and more shrilly that to understand is to misunderstand it. They try to break up the very pattern of rational discourse in order to convey their message — but the problem will not go away. For whatever kind of philosophy or criticism you write will always carry with it the implication that it emerges from, and is part of, a system, that it is possible, finally, to pin a sense on things. Even if what finally makes sense is that there is no system, no ultimate authority for sense.

For the truth of the matter is that for criticism to manifest anxiety at its own status is not at all the same thing as for art to do so. For this anxiety itself, in critical discourse, still gives off the feeling of being manipulated, of being yet another *device*. This is very different from what happens in Herbert or Proust, Dante or Virginia Woolf, where understanding is always balanced by the failure of understanding, and where the inevitable result of passing time is recognised and accepted as the source of both loss and gain. But criticism, by its very nature, however tactful or sensitive it may be, always presents us with the finished object, and it is helpless to show how it might very well not have been, or at what cost it has come to be what it is.

And this, to come back to my opening remarks, is why that off-hand, casual criticism which is to be found in the letters of artists is actually truer to our experience of art than real criticism of whatever kind — scholarly, positivist, intuitive, deconstructionist, or any combination of these. Here, in a letter, we are in no danger of mistaking the comment for the final summation. We are made to sense, not by anything the writer says or does, but by the dramatic context, that critical understanding is less an ever-expanding structure than a set of possibilities either realised or passed over. And this of course is to some extent true also of the more polemical pronouncements of artists. What we feel reading a comment by Eliot on Milton or by Stravinsky on Beethoven is that what they are saying is terribly important to them at that moment: here, now, it is vital to put down Milton or Beethoven, to draw attention to the qualities of Marvel or Haydn. Later it will be equally important to assert the importance of Milton and Beethoven once more; but this is not an example of flagrant self-contradiction so much as of the fact that later is another time, with other issues, other challenges. We are therefore not in danger of simply redrawing the map of the past in a new way; rather, we are made to recognise the implications of each emphasis. And this can only make our appreciation of a Milton or a Beethoven a deeper because a more considered thing.

And this suggests a further point: that the whole notion of individual masterpieces, of works or texts to be examined, analysed, even approved of or rejected simply on their own merit, apart from the whole corpus of the author's work, is not a natural one. It too belongs to a particular culture — what we might call the museum culture of the Renaissance to the nineteenth century. It was of course the sense of the break-up of such a culture which led to the best writing of Erich Auerbach and Walter Benjamin. But again it is the poets who have put

INTRODUCTION

it most clearly. In the second stanza of 'A Primitive Like an Orb' Wallace Stevens reminds us that our response to individual works by an artist depends on our sense of the whole of his work, and on that whole as a project rather than a universe, even though it is a project that can only be apprehended through individual works.

> We do not prove the existence of the poem.
> It is something seen and known in lesser poems.
> It is the huge, high harmony that sounds
> By little and a little, suddenly,
> By means of a separate sense. It is and it
> Is not and, therefore, is. In the instant of speech,
> The breadth of an accelerando moves,
> Captures the being, widens — and was there.

This sense of the relation of the part to the whole is, finally, what justifies my statement that it is in the letters of artists that we find the best criticism. For it is only there that the complete interconnection of part and whole, artist and achievement, is implicitly recognised and made the ground of all comment.

Yet if this is so it entails an important corollary. This is that the illumination afforded by an artist's letters will in the end depend for us on how far we trust that artist — both in his work and in these letters. Stevens and Keats say what they do and make this a cause of deep reflection because they are Stevens and Keats. I do not mean because they lived the lives they did (no two lives could have been more different, after all), but because in their poetry and their approach to poetry we sense that combination of openness and purposefulness which makes us pause and listen. Of course, there will be people for whom neither the aims nor the achievements of these two particular writers will mean very much. And such people are not necessarily either foolish or insensitive. It may be that it is other writers who strike a chord in them; and it may be that they will come to Keats and Stevens in due time. Once again, where criticism, however modest, asserts some kind of absolute truth (this is a great poet, an important work), letters never tempt us to make such an assumption. 'This is, or is not, for me, now,' is the most that they assert. And this does not mean the elevation of taste and whim at the expense of judgement. It means rather that implicit in a letter is the recognition that our response to works of art can never be separated from our entire conception of how and why we lead the lives we do.

Of course, certain critics recognise this and try to base their arguments on particular conceptions of character and particular views of life. But this is just the trouble. Doing this, they become bullies; we sense them trying to argue us into the belief that their own clear-cut notion of what reality or morality is is the only correct one. And, inevitably, we feel that too much is being left out. In a writer's letters we rarely feel that we are entering a closed system, but rather that there is always the possibility that we, like the writer himself, may always be startled by the unexpected, forced to change by events or feelings we had not expected to experience. Our relation to a volume of letters becomes itself a fluid, changing thing and, at its basis, if we are interested enough to persevere with it, there lies less the acceptance of a system than the pleasure of an encounter.

But what, it will be asked, has all this to do with a collection of reviews? For if it is true, as I have been arguing, that the critic is that much lower than the artist in his letters, then surely the reviewer is lower even than the critic. For the reviewer is the very lowest of literary hacks, a drudge who performs a job no one is quite sure he needs, and whose precise function no one can quite explain. And yet, it seems to me, in the right circumstances, reviewing can come as close as it is possible for criticism to come to the ideal I have been outlining. For the circumstances to be right the reviewer needs to be free of a weekly or fortnightly chore; he must be able to write reviews only if and when he pleases. He must also have a fair amount of room to manoeuvre in (though not too much — a word-limit sharpens the mind and prose wonderfully). And, finally, he must have imaginative editors. Given these three conditions something of interest may emerge. The reviewer may find that he encounters books he might not otherwise have read, at moments when such books are particularly meaningful to him; and, just because the form can look after itself (the external constraints of time and space see to that), the reviewer sometimes finds that he is free of inhibitions he might otherwise have had and surprises even himself.

Of course, if our trust of artists depends on what we feel about their overall performance, their integrity and the value of the goals they have set themselves, this is even truer of reviewers. We only read a reviewer with attention because he has earned that attention. And this happens all too rarely, just because it is so easy to be irresponsible in a review. (There is always the temptation to treat the constraints of time and space as excuses for irresponsibility.) But when, as in the case of an

INTRODUCTION

Auden, a Berryman, a Jarrell, we recognise that the occasional eccentricity is part of a genuine and valid vision and of a deep commitment to their art, then we listen to them with patience, even when we are not familiar with the books they are reviewing and may imagine that they hold little of interest for us.

Of course the gaining of such confidence is never a matter of the exertion of the will. Indeed, the more wilful he is, the more we feel him trying to impose himself upon us as a personality, the less we are likely to trust a reviewer. This is probably why the very successful regular reviewers, like Edmund Wilson and Kenneth Tynan, strike us in the end as a little tiresome.

I am sure I have frequently succumbed to the temptations described above. But I have always tried to write with my eye on the object and not on a public or my own performance. The reviews which follow have been selected from those I felt to be the least unsuccessful. They cover art as well as literature, the Bible and Dante as well as recent poetry and fiction. I don't believe in eclecticism for its own sake, but I don't believe in artifical barriers either. Some of the reviews were exciting to write because here was a chance to put together my ideas on an author or topic I had long felt ambivalent about — such is the piece on Graham Greene. Others were responses to topics or authors I had not previously given much thought to but which, I was delighted to discover, touched vital nerves in me — the essays on Schapiro and on Hebrew poetry are of this kind. The majority were written in the last three years, while I was working on the lectures that became *Writing and the Body*. Many of the themes, and even some of the examples, are the same as those of that book, and I tend to see this volume as the mould of which the other is the sculpture. Moulds are, to my mind, in many ways more interesting than sculptures. I have also included, to round off the volume, a piece I wrote in answer to reviews of my novels. It seemed appropriate to end with the reviewer reviewed.

Some of the essays are highly critical. Mistakes and failures are never uninteresting, they too have their roots in human nature. I hope, therefore, that I have never been critical just for its own sake but always to draw attention to temptations to which we are all subject. In the end though the reviews that are most enjoyable to write and no doubt to read are those written in response to what has moved, pleased and excited one. If the reviewer can persuade the reader to go away and read such works, then he has done his job. If he has been able to suggest why they mean a great deal to him, then he has done even better. How significant this fact is for the reader will depend in the last analysis on the reader's own assessment of the reviewer himself, and there is no way the reviewer can pre-empt that. He can only do the job as honestly and lucidly as possible. Here, as in art itself, John Berryman's prescription remains the best:

>Write as short as you can,
>In order, of what matters.

Lewes, August 1982

2

True Mastery *

No one, except perhaps Proust, has been able to express such a sense of totally unexpected joy as Dante, and what most often brings joy flooding through his body is the chance meeting with a revered ancestor or teacher. 'O sanguis meus, O superinfus gratia Dei,' Cacciaguida greets him in Paradise, and Dante, turning in puzzlement to Beatrice, feels that 'I had touched the limit both of my beatitude and of my paradise.' Then, he tells us, the spirit continues to speak, and it is 'a joy to hearing and to sight'. Many hours before, deep down in the pit of Hell, another meeting had taken place, following a very similar pattern:

> Eyed in this way by this company,
> I was recognised by one of them, who seized me
> By the edge of my cloak, and cried: 'How marvellous!'
> And, when he stretched out his arm to me,
> I fixed my eyes upon his scorched appearance
> So that his burnt face should not prevent
> The recognition of him by my intellect;
> And, bending my face towards his,
> I answered him: 'Are you here, ser Brunetto?'

'Siete voi qui, ser Brunetto?' — the poetry leaps, as does the pilgrim Dante's heart at the sight of his old teacher, even here, in the burning valleys of Hell. It is because the contact between them is so immediate and so strong, so uncluttered by doubts or second thoughts, that the last image of the canto so often quoted out of context, achieves its power:

> Then he turned back, and seemed to be one of those
> Who, at Verona, run for the green cloth,

Through the open country; and he seemed to be the one
Who wins the race, and not the one who loses.

But of course it is in the meeting with a greater master than Brunetto could ever be that we learn most fully why Dante attached so much importance to this aspect of life. It will be remembered that Dante, having come to in the dark wood, emerges and tries to climb a great mountain towards the sun, only to be pushed back by three beasts. 'While I was ruining down to the depth,' he says, using one of those frightening Dantesque words which combine the moral and physical inextricably, *rovinava*, 'there appeared before me one who seemed faint through long silence.' It is Virgil, who is faint (or hoarse) because he has been silent for thirteen centuries. But at this point Dante does not know who he is, and it is an important principle of this poem that we do not forestall the narrator with our prior knowledge, for the way the encounter unfolds between them is of crucial importance:

> When I saw that fellow in the great desert,
> I cried out to him: 'Have pity on me,
> Whatever you are, shadow or definite man.'

The figure answers, 'No, not a living man, though once I was,' and proceeds to explain that his parents were Lombards and that he himself was born under Julius Caesar and lived in Rome under the good Augustus 'at the time of the false and lying gods'. Only after he has said this does he go on to explain what he did in life: 'I was a poet, and I sang of that just son of Anchises who came from Troy after proud Ilium was burned.' At this point Dante can contain himself no longer:

> Are you then that Virgil and that fountain
> Which pours forth so rich a stream of speech...?
> O glory and light of other poets!
> May the long study avail me, and the great love
> That made me search your volume.
>
> You are my master and my author;
> You alone are he from whom I took
> The good style that has done me honour.

It is fitting that Virgil should see himself clearly, and in the harsh light of eternity the facts, in descending order of importance, are as he presents them: that he was born under the false and lying gods, which accounts for his sad place in Hell; and then that what he did in his life was to sing of a just man who escaped from a proud city (thus

TRUE MASTERY

preparing the way for that other just man who would topple the proud city of the Caesars and erect his own in Heaven). He was, of course, the supreme poet of antiquity, but for him, at this point, that is irrelevant — it would make no difference if he had been the most minor of scribblers. However, it is also right that for Dante it *should* make a difference, and it is right that he should gasp with wonder and delight: 'Or se'tu quel Virgilio e quella fonte/che spandi di parlar si largo fiume?... Tu se'lo mio maestro e'l mio autore.'

What exactly is the meaning of that last phrase? 'My author' — the one who made me, as well as my special writer. As the *Commedia* unfolds, we come to see how these two meanings interfuse and how, quite simply, without Virgil, Dante would not have been himself, for it is Virgil who allowed him to find his own voice.

This is the real mystery of 'influence'. This is what past masters, if they are true masters, have to teach those who follow them. This is what drew Eliot to Dante when he, too, was lost in a strange land and without a voice of his own, able only to mimic brilliantly the voices of others. When Virgil and Dante approach the summit of Mount Purgatory they meet a new figure, Statius, who, like Dante, has also found his voice through Virgil. Not knowing who the two pilgrims are, he recounts his life:

> I sang of Thebes, then of the great Achilles;
> But fell by the wayside with the second load.
> The seeds of my ardour were the sparks
> Which emanated from the divine flame
> By which more than a thousand have been set alight;
> I speak of the Aeneid, which was at once
> Mother and nurse to me in poetry;
> Without which I should have been worth almost nothing.
> And to have lived back there when Virgil was alive,
> I would consent readily to an extra year
> Of banishment before I am released.

Virgil motions to Dante to be silent, but Statius has already caught the beginnings of a smile on his face, and asks Dante to explain the reason. When Statius learns who it is he has been speaking to,

> Already he was stooping to embrace the feet
> Of my teacher, but the latter said: 'Do not,
> Brother, for you are a shadow and so am I.'

THE MIRROR OF CRITICISM

> And he, rising, 'Now you can understand
> The quantity of love which warms me to you,
> When I put out of mind our vanity,
> 'Treating shadows as if they were solid things.'

In 1917, an unknown American poet living in England brought out his first volume of poetry, a collection full of ironic echoes of the past and quotations from past masters, not one of which could be taken at its face value; indeed, it was difficult to know where the face or the value of the collection lay; the only thing that was clear was that a major poet had arrived, and the Romantic era was over. The title page of the volume carried a dedication in French and English and an epigraph in Italian: 'For Jean Verdenal, 1889-1915, mort aux Dardanelles', followed by those lines of Statius to Virgil:

> la quantitate
> puote veder del amor che a te mi scalda
> quando dismento nostra vanitate
> trattando l'ombre come cosa salda.

The effect is quite extraordinary. These lines, in another language, written by another poet, spoken by a third poet about a fourth, come through with a heartbreaking directness — the only direct and 'sincere' lines in the whole of *Prufrock and Other Observations*.

We can, I think, assent to the mystery without feeling any need to fathom it. But it is this quality above all others, I am convinced, which brought Eliot to Dante and kept him there all his life — Dante's profound understanding of the nature of the encounter between past and present, self and other, which cannot be explained in terms of influence or style, but ony in terms of the whole person. Our relation to the masters we choose from the past — or who seem to choose us — is partly our relation to our fathers, partly to our mothers. Throughout the *Commedia*, interestingly enough, it is Virgil who seems to assume the role of mother, even at one point carrying Dante on his hip as peasant mothers still do, while it is Beatrice who assumes the fearsome but no less essential fatherly role, rebuking Dante for his irresponsibility and lack of steadfastness.

George Holmes is a distinguished medieval historian, and his little book on Dante for the Oxford University Press 'Past Masters' series is a serious and sensible piece of work. But in another sense it is a scandal. No one reading it would ever imagine that Dante might be for him what he was for Eliot, what Virgil was for Dante. As John Dunn pointed out in an earlier number of the *London Review of Books*, this new series has never really asked itself what a past master might be, and the title seems merely to be an excuse to peddle yet more secondary works in an already overloaded market.

Holmes, in typical historian's fashion, first bows to the 'beauties' of a literary work and then gets down to the serious business of telling us what is 'important' about it. The following passage is, alas, typical:

> The *Comedy* is the most carefully wrought and the most precisely and intricately symmetrical of great literary works.... But for the reader who attempts to go beyond the exterior enjoyment of this magnificent artifice to understand its meaning and its relation to Dante's ideas, it presents an ocean of problems.

Holme's method is to try and trace the changes in Dante's 'ideas' in the course of his writing the *Comedy*, showing how different the three *cantiche* are in their assumptions and interests, and how closely the changes coincide with the changing political situation. This is quite interesting to the person who already knows and loves the poem, but what it does is break it up and destroy the complex set of relations Dante has established within it, to reduce it, in the end, to little more than an ill-organised encyclopedia. This is very much how scholars like Screech and Frame treat Rabelais, but I have never seen it so ruthlessly applied to Dante. What it does is to ensure that hardly anyone will ever go from the essay to the poem, though quite a few will no doubt feel, having read it, that they now know what Dante is 'about'.

We respond to Eliot's essay on Dante because we feel that Eliot himself is responding to Dante, that the encounter has been central to his life. Anyone who sets out to translate Dante must also have experienced some such emotion, for the road is long and the frustrations are bound to be great, and mere industriousness could hardly keep him going. To judge by his introduction, C. H. Sisson is armed, if not with love for Dante, at least with great confidence in his own abilities. Dismissing the efforts of Binyon and Dorothy Sayers ('it is not any language, though nearest, no doubt, to the quotha and forsooth of Victorian knightly romanticism'), he insists that for him the problem 'presents itself... in an entirely concrete form'. The translator, as he sees it,

> is not looking for a critical adjective which will describe how he views the matter or how he will perform; he will be fumbling for a

few lines which convince him that he can go on, and in some sort say what his poet says. That may sound a modest requirement; the rigour of it depends on the degree of rigour the translator is accustomed to exercise in relation to his own writing.

On the evidence of this, Sisson does not exercise much rigour in his own writing. His translation is so unsatisfactory, so clumsy and careless, that at times one might almost suppose that it was a rough draft snatched from his hand by an over-eager publisher.

No criticism without examples, as Nabokov said, so here goes. First, the general slackness of the language. 'This flame would stay absolutely still,' for 'would shake no more'; 'and we left him in that awkward situation,' for 'thus embroiled'; 'Your will is free, just, and as it should be,' for 'libero, dritto e sano e tuo arbitrio' (why not 'upright'?). This may be an attempt at a relaxed, colloquial style, rather like Day Lewis's version of the *Aeneid*, but it feels merely clumsy. There are, however, larger doubts about this translation. In Canto XXII of *Paradiso* Sisson has substituted 'my heart' for 'your heart' so that the passage makes no sense. He seems not to know the Italian expression for 'to faint', so translating 'io venni men cosi com'io morisse' ('I fainted as though I were dying') as 'I felt myself diminish...'. He adds clumsiness to mistranslation when he renders 'cosi rotando, ciascuno il visaggio / drizzava a me, si che'n contraro il collo / faceva ai pie continuo viaggio' (literally, as Singleton has it, 'thus each, wheeling, directed his face on me so that his neck kept turning in a direction contrary to his feet') as 'And so, as they ran round, they kept their faces / Turned all the time towards me, so that their necks / Were all the time in movement, like their feet.'

In this example, it is difficult to say if the awkwardness is due to deliberate choice or simple carelessness, for Sisson seems often to go out of his way to break up the symmetry of the poem, or to add symmetries of his own which the poem could well do without. Thus he doesn't end the first canticle with the word 'stars', though it would have been easy to do so and he keeps that ending for the other two; while, on the other hand, in his description of the siren in Canto XIX of *Purgaorio*, he repeats the loose 'washed out' twice (she had 'all her colour washed out' and then the colour came back 'to her washed-out face') where Dante has *scialba* and *smaritto*. The most awkward instance occurs in Canto XXXI of *Purgatorio*, during the climactic encounter with Beatrice: Sisson repeats 'my face' three times where Dante has first 'my face', and then 'my eye'.

TRUE MASTERY

> And when my face was raised in her direction,
> My face grasped the fact that the primal creatures...

What does it mean to say: 'My face grasped the fact...'? If Dante had used that unnatural expression there would be some justification for it, however odd it might sound in English. But he doesn't.

In the above examples, the English reader would at least be warned by the clumsiness that something was wrong with the translation. But there are occasions where Sisson has so translated key words that the entire poem is affected and no one who did not have the Italian to hand would be aware of it. Thus a central notion of the *Inferno* is that of *contrapasso*: the idea that a man's punishment fits his sin. The English word ought to be something like 'retribution', but Sisson chooses 'retaliation', which suggests a vindictive god. This is perhaps how Sisson feels about Dante's deity, but it distorts what Dante means us to understand. Much later, when Dante and Beatrice are flying through the heavens, she asks him to look down and he sees 'il varco / folle d'Ulisse' ('the mad track / of Ulysses'). This is one of the moments in the poem when the linear development is suddenly seen to be part of a spatial pattern too, and when what had seemed to be wholly disparate themes and distinct characters are seen to fit into complex relations of parallelism and opposition. Sisson throws it away by translating: 'the passage the demented Ulysses took'. But Ulysses was not demented — he was mad in the sense of being an overreacher. The passage adds to the Aeneas/Ulysses, Dante/Ulysses contrasts, and binds *Inferno* and *Paradiso* together. By not thinking enough about the meaning of the whole poem when translating a specific phrase, Sisson erodes the entire fabric.

In Dante every word is important. The more one reads him, the more obvious it becomes that, however relaxed and 'natural' the style, meaning emerges out of the constant juxtaposition, sometimes many cantos apart, of key words and phrases, images and even figures. Sisson has thrown all this away, and given us in its stead a poem in a language that is roughly like what we might speak today. Yet he keeps to the three-line stanzas, though abandoning rhyme and precise metre, and for this we must be grateful, though perhaps to the publisher more than the translator. Those clean-looking little stanzas on the large white pages slow reading down and make us aware of this as a poem, with a different pace from prose. That is a big advantage.

Reading through Sisson's translation and sampling a few others, I wondered again whether English could ever cope with Dante's particular style. It's so precise, so concrete, yet so unaggressive. Thus 'la terra lagrimosa' at the start of the *Inferno* is a tearful or tear-soaked ground, not 'the melancholy land', as Sisson would have it; and 'lascia pur grattar dov'e la rogna' is rather 'let them scratch where the itch is' than 'let them scratch wherever they may itch'. Dante is always specific and physical, and it will not do to turn his nouns into verbs or to say: 'This is the sort of thing he means.' Sisson is partly aware of this physical aspect of Dante's imagination and of its underlying violence, but his attempts to make his English correspondingly violent and harsh nearly always backfire. Thus in *Inferno* XXII we are told 'That was brother Gomita,/The one from Gallura, a bucketful of cheats,' but the original merely says 'vasel d'ogne froda' ('a vessel of every fraud'). Again, as Dante finally leaves Saturn he hears a terrible noise: 'It resembled nothing upon earth', writes Sisson, 'Nor could I understand it; the roar flattened me.' But the Italian is again effortlessly precise: 'ne io lo 'ntesi, si mi vinse il tuono' ('nor did I understand it, the thunder overcame me so').

One can see what Sisson is trying to do here: he is attempting to give physical force to his language by substituting the physical 'flattened me' for the more generalised 'overcame me'. At such moments he is going for the reverse effect of his usual drab style, and trying to write in the manner of Lowell and Heaney. And it is certainly true that these two poets have got much closer to Dante's controlled violence than any other translator I know. Lowell renders the meeting with Brunetto Latini (which I gave above in Sisson's translation): 'Soon, / I saw a man whose eyes devoured me, saying, / "This is a miracle."' And he captures wonderfully the end of Buonconte de Montefeltro: 'flying on foot and splashing the field with blood'. Heaney too, in his version of Ugolino, works wonders with the English language:

> We had already left him. I walked the ice
> And saw two soldered in a frozen hole
> On top of other, one's skull capping the other's,
> Gnawing at him where the neck and head
> Are grafted to the sweet fruit of the brain,
> Like a famine victim at a loaf of bread.
> So the berserk Tydeus gnashed and fed
> Upon the severed head of Menalippus
> As if it were some spattered carnal melon.

This is remarkable. And yet it's not quite Dante either. The line of

TRUE MASTERY

Purgatorio that Lowell renders so memorably is 'fuggendo a piede e sanguinando il piano' ('fleeing on foot and bloodying the plain'). The parallel participles give an extra terror to the image, binding together aurally what is primarily an image of dispersal — of blood, of self, of an army: so that Dante can dispense with Lowell's 'splashing with blood'. Dante's is not, as Eliot, perhaps over-impressed by Pound's half-truths, argued, a visual imagination. Its miraculous quality comes from its being both aural and visual at once, with the two not simply reinforcing each other, but sometimes, as here, powerfully at odds. Similarly, Heaney's image of 'the sweet fruit of the brain' is a brilliant solution, but Dante's is ultimately more terrifying for being less immediately startling:

> e come 'l pan per fame si manduca,
> cosi'l sovran li denti a l'alto pose
> la've'l cervel s'aggiunge con la nuca...

The quiet rhyme of *manduca* and *nuca*, picking up *buca* in the previous tercet, seems to make the cannibalism almost natural. We have no sense of Dante working up the scene to produce horror; it seems to simply exist, embedded in these words.

In his elegy for Lowell, Heaney movingly describes his friend and fellow poet as 'the master elegist/and welder of English', and goes on to ask rhetorically, 'what was not within your empery?' answering:

> You drank America
> like the heart's
> iron vodka,
>
> promulgating art's
> deliberate, peremptory
> love and arrogance.

But is this not a very partial view of art, though one undoubtedly cultivated by Lowell? The artist as predator, as emperor, deliberate, peremptory and arrogant — this is certainly the posture that seems to have worked best for poets writing in English in the last twenty years, but its willed and wilful quality suggests a desperation which is incompatible with the greatest poetry. With, for example, the poetry of Dante. For the wondrous thing about Dante is how unaggressive he is, how little we feel him to be asserting mastery over language, and yet how powerful he is. In a brilliant chapter of his book, *Dante, Poet of the Secular World*, Auerbach noted, many years ago, how much more striking are the first lines of sonnets by Dante's older contemporaries, Guinizelli and Cavalcanti, than those of Dante's own early attempts. But whereas the other two can only reiterate more and more frenziedly the effects of their openings, Dante's sonnets flower with a magical inevitability until the last word arrives as the only possible and necessary conclusion. And in the *Commedia* this combination of art and nature, of form and subject-matter, is even more evident, with the *terza rima* holding the giant edifice together, and the words *amore* and *tornare* playing a central role: for only those supple enough to turn and return, through love, rather than violently trying to force their way forward, can be saved, only they can find their own voice, for

> Per lor maladizion si non si perde
> che non possa tornar l'etterno amore,
> mentre che la speranza ha fior del verde.

['None is so lost that the eternal love can not return, so long as hope keeps aught of green.]

Only Wordsworth, in a few great moments in *The Prelude*, found a way to combine pliancy and strength in the way Dante consistently does, and Wordsworth's view of man does not allow him to deal with human love, the pleasures and pains of making and the mysteries of beneficial influence. Which is only another way of saying that if there is one master we need, now, that master is Dante.

NOTES

Dante, George Holmes, Oxford, 1980

The Divine Comedy: A New Verse Translation, C. H. Sisson, Carcanet, £8.95, 1980

1 Extended quotations from Dante in the early part of this article are given in C. H. Sisson's translation, except for the passage which begins 'Are you then that Virgil...', which is based on the Dent translation.

3

What Was Chaucer Really Up To?*

————▶◆●◆◆◀————

I

>   Listeth, lordes, in good entent,
>   And I wol telle verrayment
>   Of myrthe and of solas;
>   Al of a knyght was fair and gent
>   In bataille and in tourneyment,
>   His name was sire Thopas.
>   Yborn he was in fer contree
>   In Flaundres, al biyonde the see,
>   At Poperyng, in the place.
>   His fader was a man full free,
>   And lord he was of that contree,
>   As it was Goddes grace.

It takes a great poet to write poetry as bad as this. In twelve lines Chaucer has already succeeded in making us lose all further interest in the deeds of his hero. No wonder Harry Bailly, the Host of the Tabard Inn, who has accompanied the pilgrims on their way to Canterbury and taken it upon himself to act as Master of Ceremonies, interrupts him with: 'Namoore of this, for Goddes dignitee... Myn eres aken of thy drasty speche.' The question for us is: How are we to take it? Why is it spoken? Is it merely a parody of second-rate romances, or is such parody, as in Cervantes, only the symptom of a larger unease? Once we open ourselves to such questions others come pouring in: Who is speaking this? The pilgrim Chaucer? The poet? (But who is the poet?) Where is it spoken? On the road to Canterbury? In our heads? Then? Now?

Chaucer is one of the great unread writers of world literature. It is true that he is the Father of English literature, but outside of English departments, where the feeling I suppose is that if you are going out with the daughters you've got to be civil to the father, one does not imagine anyone reading him or having any particular incentive to do so. Dryden's remark that 'here is God's plenty', though meant as a term of praise, would seem designed to put one off rather than encourage one to sample. Who wants God's plenty nowadays, especially if it's in verse and in a slippery language that at moments looks just like English and then turns suddenly into gibberish? But perhaps he has more to say to us than we often realise, perhaps he is more puzzling, doubting, inquiring, than the traditional image of him suggests. All we need to do is open his poems and see for ourselves. This, in their various ways, is what all the books under review urge us to do . Some, however, are more persuasive than others, and it may be of some theoretical as well as of practical interest to see just why this should be so.

The great merit of John Gardner's books is that they clearly set out to convert: 'I write about Chaucer', he says, 'because I believe profoundly what he says in his poetry about human life, and believe his ideas are more significant right now, in the twentieth century, than they ever were before, even in his own century.' His assets are enormous enthusiasm for anything connected with Chaucer and a boundless confidence in his own ability to convey that enthusiasm. The results, however, are disappointing.

Let us begin with the biography. Here, right at the start, Gardner runs into difficulties. For the fact is that very little is known about Chaucer. We have no letters, no memoirs, no way of knowing what Chaucer thought or what his contempories thought about him in private. Since he was a civil servant for most of his life there are plenty of records, but these never once mention poetry or even writing. Thus Gardner is reduced to filling out his book with potted intellectual and political history: the troubles of Edward II, medieval attitudes to children, the course of Edward III's French wars, the medieval school curriculum, fourteenth-century Oxford, Ockham, Wycliffe, Alice Perrers, The Peasants' Revolt, etc. When the going gets a little heavy he brings in a bit of 'human interest': Did John of Gaunt have an affair with his sister-in-law, Chaucer's wife? Was Chaucer's son really Gaunt's? What exactly did Chaucer do to incur the charge of *raptus* (rape or abduction) — this in 1380, when he was a middle-aged, happily married man? The evidence here, as elsewhere, is inconclusive.

WHAT WAS CHAUCER REALLY UP TO?

The trouble with all this is not so much that there is a great deal we can never know; it is that even the things we can be reasonably certain about seem to cast little light on the man, the poet, or the age. Gardner points out at the start that where there are gaps in knowledge he will frequently be forced to use 'the novelist's prerogative' to invent, but though this makes the book more readable, in the end it does Chaucer a disservice. We are very conscious of having Gardner's Chaucer, rather than Chaucer himself, Gardner's version of the English fourteenth century rather than any insight into what the period was really like. It is true that we learn a few facts on the way — it was, for example, 'legal to beat a wife into unconsciousness, but not acceptable to beat her until her inert body farted, a sign that she was in shock and might possibly be dying'[1] — but these remain isolated and fragmentary. By the end we are no nearer to Chaucer or his age than when we started.

The Poetry of Chaucer is equally disappointing, though here it is harder to put one's finger on the source of failure. 'I have no single point to make about Chaucer's poetry', Gardner says at the start, 'except of course that it is a joy to read, a magnificent, puzzling, delightful world to move into.' His method is to begin at the beginning, with *The Book of the Duchess*, and to work his way through the canon to the Retraction at the end of *The Canterbury Tales*. He has read much of the recent scholarship on Chaucer, and there are many good insights on the way, usually culled (with ample acknowledgement) from the work of others. But my overall impression of the book is that it is at once too dense and too thin. Gardner's answer would no doubt be that the book is meant to be an introduction for the general reader: 'In a book meant for non-specialists,' he says at the start of his discussion of the *Canterbury Tales*, 'it would be impossible to present a full line-by-line analysis of the whole work, much less a full appreciation of its magnificence as poetry.' But does this distinction not rest on a strange assumption? Is the difference between a book for the general reader and one for 'specialists' really that between general comments and line-by-line analysis? Though Gardner constantly gestures in the direction of scholarship he hives it off from 'response to the poetry' with a positively ruthless determination: 'It is not my purpose', he declares in the preface,

> to write a book closely examining Chaucer's possible use of the writings of Robert Grosseteste, or Chaucer's relationship to John

THE MIRROR OF CRITICISM

Gower, or the influence of Livy on Chaucer's aesthetic theory. My purpose is to follow where the poems lead, avoiding presuppositions but turning to ideas popular in Chaucer's day when those ideas seem to illuminate the poem.

Are these really the alternatives? Part of the trouble would seem to be that it is very hard to write an interesting book which has *no* particular point to make. Our sense of the book's diffuseness and lack of bite stems perhaps from Gardner's initial decision about the kind of book he wanted to write. But this is not the whole reason, for Gardner does in fact, despite his early disclaimer, have a 'point' or thesis, and it is one he drives rather hard. Chaucer, he argues, lived in a period which saw the triumph of Nominalism, and he sensed therefore that all truth is relative 'and knew that quite possibly, there can be, in the end, no real communication between human beings'. This, it seems, links him with 'Samuel Beckett and many other writers of the first rank in this century', who have also played with 'the paradox of speech denying the validity of speech'.

This is a strange argument. Though Chaucer does undoubtedly deal in his later works with problems of language and communication it seems odd to relate this exclusively to a scholastic controversy. Is it not more likely that Nominalism too is the response to profound and complex transformations in medieval society in the later Middle Ages? However, that is not the point I want to labour. I don't feel it's the oddness of Gardner's thesis or the general flaccidity of the language in which he presents it ('Samuel Beckett and many other writers of the first rank in this century') that is the primary reason for our dissatisfaction with his book; it has to do rather with the kinds of question he asks of Chaucer's text.

Here is where Alfred David's book can help us, if only negatively. For he does definitely have a thesis — indeed, he sets out to do little else than argue this thesis — and yet it leaves us with the same feelings as Gardner's book: we are left at the end with the sense that the pieces have been energetically moved about on the board, but that in reality nothing has changed.

David's thesis is oddly old-fashioned, though he too makes full use of the most recent scholarship. Briefly, he argues that Chaucer began his career with the notion of the poet as preacher which was prevalent in his time, and ended it by divorcing his fiction completely from the

WHAT WAS CHAUCER REALLY UP TO?

domination of morality. The turning point, according to David, is to be found in the General Prologue to *the Canterbury Tales*:

> Chaucer's Prologue... is liable to the charge that, by medieval standards, it is not moral enough because it fails to make judgement explicit. By modern standards, that is its greatness as a work of art. Great fiction has the power of making the reader suspend moral judgement along with the sense of disbelief. He becomes absorbed in the imaginary characters *for their own sake* and not for the sake of some truth or moral that can be learned from them.

This is just a more sophisticated version of the old argument that Chaucer gradually broke free of the shackles of medieval conventions and found a way to write about 'real life'. David compares Chaucer's achievement with Boccaccio's but one just has to look at *The Canterbury Tales* and *The Decameron* to see the error of such a view: Boccaccio's elegant young people are cocooned from the world; they tell their tales in a vacuum, and they themselves have, in a sense, no past. Chaucer sets his characters on a pilgrimage to Canterbury, and neither their own pasts nor the culture in which they are embedded can be cast off: the book is in one sense precisely about the interrelation of the two, of individual and society, the modern and the ancient, freedom and tradition.

But again, it is not so much the errors of David's thesis that need to be established as the weakness of the questions he asks of Chaucer. Perhaps what he says is true; perhaps it isn't. Either way it seems to make little difference. But, it may be asked: Is there any kind of criticism or scholarship which *does* make a difference? I think there is, and, rather than arguing my case in a theoretical way, I would like to place alongside the three works I've looked at a couple of others which will make my point for me.

In 1960 J. V. Cunningham published an essay entitled 'Convention as Structure: The Prologue to *The Canterbury Tales*', in a book called *Tradition and Poetic Structure*. In it he pointed out that the pilgrimage to Canterbury was undoubtedly a common occurrence in Chaucer's day, and that 'he had in all likelihood seen a good many groups of pilgrims among whom were to be found close analogues to the characters in the Prologue' (cf. Gardner: 'It was probably during this period too that he came to know well those country types he would immortalise in *The Canterbury Tales*.') But where scholars had been concerned to establish that Chaucer lived in Greenwich on the

THE MIRROR OF CRITICISM

Canterbury Road or even went on pilgrimage himself, Cunningham wants to establish something quite different:

> The argument is that what he found day after day in real life he needed no literary precedent to invent. But this is not so. It is not the direct observation of murders and of the process of detection that leads to the construction of a detective story. Nor was it the perception of violent death in high places that prompted the Elizabethan dramatist to compose a tragedy. What a writer finds in real life is to a large extent what his literary tradition enables him to see and to handle.

With this essential principle in mind, Cunningham goes on to discover a model for the Prologue in a number of medieval works: in *The Romance of the Rose*, in Gower's *Confessio Amantis*, and in Chaucer's own early dream vision poems. In all of these, as in the Prologue, we can discern a number of constant elements: the poem is set in a specific season, usually Spring; the season is often described; the author, usually as dreamer, is a character in his own poem; he comes to a place — field, palace or inn — where he sees a series of portraits or a group of people; these are then described, panel fashion; whereupon one of the group, or a new character, initiates the main action, sometimes by proposing that a series of tales be related.

Now why is such an account so immediately exciting? First of all, I think, because it recognises a central fact about artistic practice. Art, even an art that deals with characters and situations we can believe in, is never a natural activity. It is the result of selection, choice, adjustment. Literary criticism that is committed to a 'realist' aesthetic chooses to ignore this, just as the novel itself ignores or hides its origins at the writer's desk. But that is itself a *feature* of 'realist' art, perhaps its most essential one. An approach like Cunningham's does not belittle Chaucer's achievement by denying its absolute originality or novel-ty; on the contrary, it makes it possible for us, for the first time, to understand how amazing that achievement really is.

But the question: 'What model did Chaucer have in mind for the Prologue?' has not yet exhausted its value. Cunningham proceeds to point out that if we look at the whole of Fragment A of *The Canterbury Tales* (The Prologue and the tales of the Knight, the Miller, the Reeve, and the Cook's fragment, with their various linking passages) we can find a model for *its* shape too in an earlier work of Chaucer's. For, after the Prologue, the Host starts the Knight off with his tale and then asks

WHAT WAS CHAUCER REALLY UP TO?

the Monk, as the leading representative of the next estate, the Clergy, to follow it up. The Miller, however, rudely interrupts and forces the company to listen to *his* tale instead. Now if we look at *The Parliament of Fowles* with this sequence in mind we find there that Nature opens the Parliament and orders the birds to speak in order of rank. This they proceed to do until suddenly the lower orders break in, crying 'Have don, and lat us wende!.../ Whan shall youre cursede pletynge have an ende?' Until then the subject had been courtly love; now a very different view of love 'is urged by a vigorous churlish personality amid a certain amount of general uproar'.

Cunningham's point seems to me to be established beyond doubt. But it is more than a 'point'. He has alerted us to aspects of Chaucer's art which had been thrust into the shadows by the 'realist' assumptions of previous critics. He has done this in a short essay with very little line-by-line analysis. Rather, sensing what questions to ask, he has made the poem and Chaucer's achievements come alive for us.

Donald R. Howard's *The Idea of the Canterbury Tales* sets out to do for the whole work what Cunningham had sketched out for a small portion of it. Howard wants us to start by taking seriously the possibility that what we have here is neither a random collection nor a small fragment of some mighty work we can only guess at, but a precisely planned work of art with only one or two minor elements missing or still to be worked out. He askes us to try to understand *what happens to us* as we read the book, and he realises that this means using all the available means of scholarship to try to understand *how it came to be*. This means not just grasping how Chaucer put it together, but why he should ever have thought of such a thing in the first place.

After arguing persuasively that the medieval notion of a pilgrimage was always of a one-way affair (no one was interested in what you did once you had reached the holy place), and thus establishing that the book has the beginning and end Chaucer meant it to have, he proceeds to a detailed comparison of some of the key elements of *Troilus* and *The Canterbury Tales*. He contrasts, for example, Chaucer's insistence on the past tense in *Troilus* with his use of the present in the *Tales*: 'This circumstance —' he says,

> that we are present *in the work* as hearers or readers — is expressed in a passage whose temporal relationships are remarkable:
>
> > *The Miller* is *a cherl, ye know well this*;
> > *So* was *the Reeve eek and othere mo,*

THE MIRROR OF CRITICISM

And harlotrie they tolden bothe two.
Avyseth you, and put me out of blame;
And eek men shall nat make ernest of game.

Why in these lines is the past tense used of the Reeve, the present tense of the Miller? — because the Miller is there at hand about to tell his tale. It is as if the narrator were watching with us.... Addressing us parenthetically, he removes (so to speak) the mask of the Miller, which he is about to put on again — holds the mask at arm's length as he pauses to comment. It is one of the most extraordinary moments in medieval literature.

Howard does not analyse the passage in detail. He only picks on the salient point for his purposes: the use of the tenses. He then proceeds to make us aware of its implications, and of the extraordinary nature of what Chaucer has done. (He rightly will have no truck with reductionist arguments of the kind: 'But who would notice this if it was read aloud?' or: 'This is too subtle for the average reader.' It's there and it's up to us to notice. The critic's task is to turn an average reader into a good one.) Again and again he sharpens our awareness by the use of comparison and contrast: 'In the *Troilus* the book is in the narrator's hand: he draws his material from it, and directs us. In *The Canterbury Tales* the book is put in our hands to make of it what we will.'

But, like Cunningham, his most potent weapon is the revelation of different possibilities, paths Chaucer might have taken but did not. He points out, for example, how much of what actually went on in pilgrimages is left out by Chaucer: we know that pilgrims sang songs on the way, but we are only given tales; the shrines where pilgrims habitually stopped on the road to Canterbury are never mentioned; pilgrimages had certain rituals of prayer and blessing, but these are ignored by Chaucer. 'Chaucer *chose*, then, to overlook some kinds of "historical" or "realistic" detail in his account of the pilgrimage in order to focus' on what was necessary for his purposes. Again, although pilgrimages would have passed through a number of towns on their way to the holy place, Chaucer takes care to start his particular one *outside* London and to end it *outside* Canterbury; he often mentions towns they pass close to, but he never has the pilgrims actually enter a town in the course of their journey. This is surely a remarkable fact, as remarkable as the things he chose to include.

Howard has explanation for all this, not all of them equally convincing. He raises far more questions than he can answer, throws

WHAT WAS CHAUCER REALLY UP TO?

out far more ideas than he quite knows what to do with: that the whole book is a 'book of memory'; that the basic design is that of the interlacing we find in fourteenth-century English illuminated manuscripts and in the Arthurian Romances; that the formal model is that of the labyrinth, itself a substitute, when inscribed on the floors of churches, as at Chartres, for actual pilgrimage.

I remain sceptical about a good many of his conclusions. His detailed treatment of individual tales is often less penetrating than Gardner's or David's. But none of this matters. His book is a vindication of the alliance between criticism and scholarship, and of the work of Chaucer. Though his book would presumably be described as aimed at specialists, it is far more likely to make anyone into whose hands it falls start reading Chaucer than Gardner's overtly popularising books. And those who already thought they knew *The Canterbury Tales* will be sent back to that book eager to read it again as it should be read — from the first word to the last.

II

I have talked about a difference in the kinds of question asked by Gardner and David on the one hand, and by Cunningham and Howard on the other. Critical methods do not exist in the void, however, and there is an historical dimension to the differences in approach which should not be overlooked. For the fact is that, of all the books under review, none except Howard's takes the Middle Ages seriously enough. I don't mean that Howard is solemn about them; only that he alone seems to be aware of the complexity and richness of the culture, and of the manifold problems of understanding it, since it is so different from our own. The others invariably treat this period as something immediately graspable.

For Woods it is a dark, dreary, restricting environment — 'the brackish backwater of medieval England', 'the rickety feudal world of the North' — into which Chaucer brought the light and gaiety he had found in Italy. For David and Gardner there is a clear gap between the stern, moralistic, 'official' view of Church and State, and the free, fun-loving openness of 'the people'. Gardner, indeed, seems to see late medieval England as a kind of rosy version of rural America more than fifty years ago: 'Make Middle-English open-hearted, like Mark Twain's jokes,' he urges in his 'Appendix on Pronunciation'.

Both David and Gardner are reacting to that school of Chaucer criticism known as 'historical' or 'exegetical', and best represented by D. W. Robertson's *A Preface to Chaucer*. The claim made by this school is that medieval culture was indeed moral, as David suggests, but that, far from reacting to this, Chaucer in fact always wrote according to its tenets. We thus get the curious situation whereby Robertson and his followers take the Nun's Priest at his word when he ends his tale by saying:

> *For seint Paul seith that al that writen is,*
> *To oure doctrine it is ywrite, ywis;*
> *Taketh the fruyt, and lat the chaf be stille.*

while David would argue that, on the contrary, the point of the tale is that we must take the chaff of the fiction and forget the fruit of moral doctrine. Both groups thus opt for a singular explanation, ignoring the obvious fact that it is the conflict between the two views that is Chaucer's primary concern.[2]

To see Chaucer as firmly part of the Middle Ages does not mean reducing his work to a series of moral platitudes. On the contrary, it means recognising that he lived in a culture so radically different from our own that it cannot simply be grasped through the deployment of formulas. To over-simplify, whereas for us the raw flux of experience contains no meaning until we impose meaning upon it, for the Middle Ages the world and everything in it had *inherent* meaning, since it had been created by God and its value guaranteed by the Incarnation.

The difference such a view makes is enormous. It is as though Chaucer and his age lived on a different planet from ours, with different laws of motion and gravity. We cannot simply wipe that difference away, or substitute for our immediate response a code extracted from two or three authors like St Augustine or St Thomas. What we need to do is to open ourselves to the variety, complexity, and alienness of the period, to grasp what such assumptions implied, even to a radical doubter like Chaucer, for his doubts were doubts *about* such a world.

As V. A. Kolve says in an important article,[3] 'We must move towards some accuracy of medieval imagining — "imaging" — at all levels.' To do this it is not enough to grasp the physical details of Chaucer's England — the clothes people wore, the sights they saw, the size of their villages and towns. We need rather to make the anthropologist's effort to grasp the whole of an alien culture with its complex set of relationships, none of which can be apprehended apart from the rest. Not to do this is, in the well-worn example, like watching a game being played but not knowing the rules; one will see as much as someone who does know the rules, but in another sense one will not see anything at all.

Historians, as well as literary critics like Howard and Kolve, are beginning to understand this. Charles Phythian-Adams, for example, in a fascinating article, 'Ceremony and the Citizen: The Communal Year at Coventry, 1450-1550',[4] remarks:

> Hocktide games took place 'in' the city and not on adjacent waste ground; maypoles stood over the streets, bonfires burnt on them; 'pageants' trundled through them.... Such practices are only a reminder that medieval streets were as important for recreation and marketing as for communication; rites and processions, like the carriage through the streets of the Corpus Christi host or the Midsummer fire, periodically added a mystical dimension to the utilitarian valuation of the immediate topographical context. While doing so, they underlined further the physical inescapability of communal involvement.

At the Reformation all this was destroyed. Not only was the spiritual life turned inward, but cultural life was too: from the streets into the churches and houses, from narration into books. The physical world, space itself, was desacralised, and the sacred found refuge only in the immaterial.

We are of course still living in that post-Reformation world. This is what makes it so important and at the same time so difficult to understand the Middle Ages. We need to develop a wholly different sense of space and time. But this is where art can help us. Medieval art does in one sense speak very directly to us. We need to learn how to translate what we instinctively feel about it into conceptual discourse, and this the scholar-critic can help us to do. With Chaucer, however, there are particular problems partly because he has for so long been looked at through Renaissance spectacles, and partly because his irony is always so difficult to gauge.

Even Howard blurs something of Chaucer's uniqueness in his excitement at bringing back for us long-forgotten modes of reading. For example, one of his central theses is that *The Canterbury Tales* is a 'book of memory', and that memory is embodied in it as a central fiction and as the controlling principle of its form: 'The expressed idea of the work is that the pilgrim Chaucer, like the pilgrim Dante of the *Commedia*, reports on an experience of his own which includes stories told by others. Both are returned travellers, both rely on memory.' And again, later: 'If we see the structure of the work in this way, there *is* something like a return journey: we are asked to read the Parson's Tale and then turn about and go over the tales again in memory, see them anew from a better perspective.... The work remembered makes us change our estimate of the work experienced.'

But does the analogy really hold? In Dante, as in Proust (also mentioned by Howard), memory is linked to *discovery*: you sink down into yourself and find there once again the plenitude of the human body as absolute potential. In Dante this work of memory is the work of the poem itself, but it is underpinned by the belief that man is made in God's image and that Christ enjoined on us to take the sacrament *in memory* of his own sacrificial action. In Chaucer, on the other hand, memory remains fragmented and we never attain a better perspective, for each change of point of vantage leads to a blotting out of the previous point. We are left with a memory perhaps, but a memory of a set of babbling voices, each squabbling for priority, each insisting on its own version of reality as the only one. In Langland, Chaucer's contemporary, the Field Full of Folk where the poem starts is called to memory by another, later field, where a joust takes place: it is Christ come to fight the devil in Piers' armour, *humana natura*. And the poet wakes from his dream of this action with the bells ringing out, summoning him to mass on Easter Day. In Chaucer no one image subsumes the others under it — the gap remains constant between meaning and event.

This difference between Chaucer and the other great medieval poets with whom he nevertheless has much in common Howard senses, as indeed do Gardner and David. They all feel that in his last works Chaucer was doing something very strange indeed. 'The idea,' Gardner says, '... that art is futile ... will become increasingly important in *The Canterbury Tales* .... Unreliable narrators one after another force us to face the question squarely, ultimately casting such doubt on art's validity as to bring on Chaucer's Retraction.' David compares the Retraction to Kafka's and Virgil's wish that their work should be burned at their death. Howard is equally eloquent:

> We know that the artist is meretricious, that his art is a bag of tricks, that his intent is to hoodwink. He is a clown and a swindler, and in

the end he is silenced like the Manciple's crow. It is going to be the same at the end of *The Canterbury Tales*: the artist is going to silence himself, retract his 'endytings of worldly vanities'. There isn't any point to all this storytelling if you are looking for the truth, because the truth lies elsewhere — lies in 'auctoritee' and finally lies in God.

But isn't there a confusion here? Kafka asked that *all* his work be burned; the Retraction is a typical medieval document, asking as it does for the author's *immoral* works not to be taken into account at the final reckoning. It cannot be used as proof of Chaucer's doubts about art in general, for his moral tales are just as much art as his fabliaux or his *Troilus*. On the other hand, if we do take the Pardoner seriously the conclusion is not necessarily that 'whereof we cannot speak thereof we must be silent'. In fact it is the Wittgenstein of the *Investigations* rather than of the *Tractatus* who should be invoked here. For Chaucer, living in an age of change and disruption, when the entire fabric of society was cracking just enough for gaps to show between the separate segments, but when the shape of the whole was still present to men's consciousness — Chaucer realised instinctively that anything we say or do falls into a pattern which is conditioned by a multitude of assumptions, most of them unconscious.

In other words, there is a Knightly ideology, as well as a Clerkly one, a feminist as well as plebian one. Moreover, all narrative, all forms of expression, have their own ideology, no matter how 'true to life' they are. Nothing is exempt, not the Knight's noble tale or the Host's violent outburst against the Pardoner, not the Parson's prose or even the Retraction itself. 'Burn off my rusts and my deformities,' Donne was to beg his God two centuries later, 'Restore thine Image, so much, by thy Grace / That thou may'st know me, and I'll turn my face.'

Chaucer remains aware of the Romantic folly of this desire. (Donne, it must be said, is half-aware of it too.) He has engaged with words and words can never bring him to the Truth. They are all tainted, contaminated, we can never make them our own. They can, however, if used with sufficient care, create a space where, in the interstices of speech, Truth can be made manifest. And I am not just thinking of the clash of tale with tale, but of the sudden lurches, hesitations, intrusions of other voices, within the tales themselves; of the sense, very evident in the Tale of Sir Thopas from which I quoted at the start, that there are innumerable ways of stringing speech together and no hint anywhere of how best to do it. Left to ourselves, as Chaucer is in that

THE MIRROR OF CRITICISM

tale, we are certain to flounder; but the old authorities are hidden or else reveal themselves in such profusion that we are at a loss to know which one to turn to. The moral of 'my dame' in the Manciple's Tale is that God gave us all two rows of teeth to show that we ought to keep our tongues firm prisoners inside our mouths. But a little earlier the Manciple had pointed out that it is as mad to try to keep a young wife locked up as it is to try to keep a bird in a cage. Everyone knows that speech is the prerogative of man, what differentiates him from the animals (who don't have it) and the angels (who don't need it). And speech, like any of the goods of this world, can be either used or misused. The responsible artist is the one who is aware of the inevitable failure of all language, its narrow ideological base, and who uses his art to bring this out into the open. In Chaucer, even in so superficially silly a piece as the Tale of Sir Thopas, the space of narration is alive as a space where writer and reader confront the temptations of language and where they learn both that we must use language if we are to remain human and that language can never lead us directly to the truth.

NOTES

*The Life and Times of Chaucer, John Gardner, Knopf, $12.50

The Poetry of Chaucer, John Gardner, Southern Illinois University Press, $15.00

The Strumpet Muse: Art and Morals in Chaucer's Poetry, Alfred David, Indiana University Press, $15.00

The Idea of the Canterbury Tales, Donald R. Howard, University of California Press, $15.00

England in the Age of Chaucer, William Woods, Stein & Day, $10.00

Chaucer: Sources and Backgrounds, ed. Robert P. Miller, Oxford University Press, $15.00; $7.00 (paper)

1 Gardner does not say where he got this piece of information from. Throughout he quotes mainly from secondary sources, and only a handful of them at that. William Woods, on the other hand, in *England in the Age of Chaucer* makes excellent use of primary sources, and conveys a remarkable sense of what it was like to be very poor in a still largely feudal society. Unfortunately his book degenerates in its later chapters into a rather simpleminded description of the political upheavals of the latter part of the century.

WHAT WAS CHAUCER REALLY UP TO?

2 Robert P. Miller's *Chaucer: Sources and Backgrounds* is a fine example of the strengths and weaknesses of documents of the exegetical school. It is a splendidly varied collection of documents and extracts, some from very well-known sources, such as Dante's *Letter to Can Grande*, others from relatively unknown sources, like Ramon Lull's *The Book of the Order of Chivalry*. All the extracts are usefully annotated and cross-referenced to the works of Chaucer. However, to give the passage in St Augustine where, discussing figurative language, he employs the image of the fruit and the chaff or the kernel and the husk, and then to direct one to the end of the Nun's Priest's Tale without pointing out the complex range of ironies involved in Chaucer's use of the idea is not just negligent, it is misleading. Still, so long as one recognises the editor's biases this is a very useful and informative book — apart from Howard's the most valuable to the reader of Chaucer of all those under review.

3 V. A. Kolve, 'Chaucer and the Visual Arts', in *Geoffrey Chaucer*, ed. Derek Brewer (London, 1974). Kolve is currently working on a book on Chaucer's narrative images which should do much to further our understanding of Chaucer.

4 In *Crisis and Order in English Towns, 1500-1700*, ed. P. Clark and P. Slack (London, 1972).

4

Reading the Middle Ages *

The life of books is a mysterious thing. If an author is still read fifty years after his death there is a strong likelihood that he will be read five centuries from then. Chaucer, at any rate, has never been far from the consciousness of readers of English, and if the last twenty years have seen an amazing upsurge of interest in him in academic circles, this has fortunately not been balanced by his disappearance from the consciousness of the wider public.

Here, as if to prove the point, is a study of Chaucer's Knight, the first of the Canterbury pilgrims to be described, by a member of the Monty Python team, Terry Jones. Jones obviously enjoys reading Chaucer, and his book conveys a personal excitement usually missing from academic studies. From the time he first came across the description of the Knight, he tells us, he was struck by the oddity of it. Why does Chaucer take thirty-six lines to describe the Knight when he could have made his point in eight? Jones began to read what historians had to say about the various battles in which the Knight is supposed to have fought, and he gradually became convinced that the conventional account of him as one of the few pilgrims to be presented non-ironically, the perfect representative of one of the three Great Orders (Commons, Clergy, Knights) into which medieval theorists divided society, was simply wrong. The Knight was in fact one of the new breed of ruthless mercenaries emerging in the later fourteenth century, men like Sir John Hawkwood, the leader of the legendary White Company, whose monument can still be seen in the Duomo in Florence next to Dante's, who hired themselves out to petty tyrants, and brought terror and destruction wherever they went. Moreover, Jones argues, Chaucer's audience would have recognised this right away: it is only we who have lost the ability to read the clues Chaucer lays before us.

Jones brings an avalanche of facts to the defence of his thesis. He has made himself master of Middle-English syntax, of the modes of construction of medieval castles, the kinds of armour worn by knights, and of the entire military history of the epoch. With the gusto of a nineteenth-century autodidact he builds up a powerful picture of the new breed of fighters who were gradually supplanting the old feudal knights with their oaths of allegiance to their lords and their complex chivalric lore. How much this portrait fits Chaucer's Knight, though, is another matter. Because every detail is turned by Jones into evidence in favour of his thesis, one gradually loses faith in him: he could just as easily, one feels, have argued in the same way even if Chaucer's description had been quite different. To take just one example, Jones makes the point again and again that men like Sir John Hawkwood infested Europe in the wake of the Hundred Years War. Whenever England and France patched up a peace, the mercenaries suddenly found themselves without pay and with nothing to do. No wonder everyone, from the Pope down, breathed a sigh of relief when they were invited to go off and deploy their skills in North Africa or Eastern Europe. But Jones also argues that Chaucer deliberately did not make his Knight fight in France, in order to show that he would not even defend his country in time of need. But surely Jones has given us a very good reason for Chaucer doing that: it was precisely to preserve the Knight from any suspicion of being one of the veteran mercenaries of the Hundred Years War. In reading this book, I was reminded of those scholarly and passionate studies of the Gospels, which are enormously convincing for the first fifty pages, about which one starts to have doubts by page 100, and which one throws away in disgust by page 150, since there is clearly no evidence which the author would not be able to turn to his advantage.

Like such books, this one has no sense of *tone*. Despite the wealth of information, I cannot reconcile Jones' picture with my reading of Chaucer. Now it may be, as Jones would certainly argue, that this is just prejudice on my part: this is how I have always seen the Knight, and I'm unwilling to change my mind. Tone is always a difficult thing to discuss, and an impossible thing to prove. Yet it is not wholly subjective either. The Knight, for example, is at once described as 'a worthy man'. Jones points out that the word is used to describe a number of other pilgrims, some of whom, like the Friar, Chaucer clearly disapproves of. But one cannot fail to be struck by the difference in tone. First, the Knight:

> A Knyght ther was, and that a worthy man,
> That fro the tyme that he first bigan
> To riden out, he loved chivalrie,
> Trouthe and honour, fredom and curteisie.

Then, the Friar:

> He knew the taverns wel in every toun
> And everich hostiler and tappestere
> Bet than a lazar or a beggestere;
> For unto swich a worthy man as he
> Accorded nat, as by his facultee,
> To have with sike lazars aqueyntance.
> It is nat honest, it may nat avaunce,
> For to deelen with no swich poraille,
> But al with riche and selleres of vitaille.

Ther is an impersonal authority in the description of the Knight, which is maintained throughout. But there is something funny about the description of the Friar. The twists and turns of the language suggest someone speaking, and we sense without needing to be told that that someone is none other than the Friar himself. It is he who describes himself as 'worthy', just as it is he who argues to the naïvely attentive Chaucer that 'it is nat honest' to have dealings with the poor, for the simple reason that 'it may nat avaunce'. Nor are we unduly surprised at the change, for the naïve pilgrim Chaucer, who generates the irony, emerges gradually in the course of the General Prologue. He is not there when the poem opens; he is definitely there when he reports in connection with one of the Monk's most outrageous remarks: 'And I seyde his opinion was good.' But is he already there in the description of the Prioress?

Irony is a tricky subject to deal with. To argue that the Knight is *not* presented ironically we may need more evidence than the mere juxtaposition of two uses of a single word. Such evidence, however, is there in abundance, though Jones chooses to ignore it. The Knight is the first of the pilgrims to be described; he is the first to be offered the 'cut' by the Host to see who will start the stories off; and, whether by chance, Chaucer says, or by destiny, it is he who picks the shortest 'cut' and so is asked to begin, whereupon the assembled pilgrims were all, we are told, 'ful blithe and glad'. The only other characters in the General Prologue who appear to be presented unironically are the

Parson and his brother the Plowman, and the book ends with the Parson agreeing to give the last tale, and

> Upon this word we han assented soone,
> For, as it seemed, it was for to doone,
> To enden in some vertuous sentence.

One further bit of evidence: when the Host, who is supposed to be the arbiter of the game of tales, falls into a bitter quarrel with the Pardoner, it is the Kight who steps forward and reconciles them, reminding them that 'as we diden, let us laugh and pleye'.

The Canterbury Tales is a notoriously problematic work. It is obviously unfinished; the pilgrims are occasionally given the wrong tales to tell; the MSS cannot agree on the right order of the tales; and some of them, like Chaucer's own tale of Melibee or the Parson's concluding treatise on sin and repentance, are so hard for us to take that even with the greatest effort of the historical imagination it is difficult to reconcile their presence with what else we know of Chaucer. But even so, it is less like *Edwin Drood* or Nietzsche's *Will to Power* than like one of those great medieval churches whose main outlines can still be seen, though portions have crumbled here and there, and whole sections may never have been started. Can it really be a coincidence that the three apparently unironic descriptions in the General Prologue are those of the representatives of the three Great Orders or Estates? Can it be a coincidence that the Knight and Parson begin and end the work, the latter explicitly linking the pilgrimage to St Thomas's shrine with that other pilgrimage we all have to make to the heavenly Jerusalem? The critic who wants to cast doubt on such points needs to do more than amass facts: he needs to provide us with an alternative theory of the general 'idea' of the work.

David Aers is altogether more ambitious and more theoretically self-aware than Terry Jones, but he too rides a hobby-horse too hard, and in the process grows deaf to tone. Aers' central argument is that great poets often speak truer than they know. Langland and, to some extent, Chaucer, accepted the dominant views of their age, but their curiosity and honesty led them to describe a world far more complex, shifting and dynamic than the simple received models would allow. Aers contrasts what he calls reflexive and non-reflexive characters in Chaucer. The Wife of Bath and, especially, the Pardoner are examples of the former: they question, either through what they say or what they do, the assumptions of the time, and the Pardoner for one is well aware of the limitations of his own views. The Knight and the Parson are examples of the latter: wooden characters whom Chaucer explicitly criticises for failing to see that their utterances are the products of a specific class and institution, and in no way the natural or universal truths they imagine them to be. His view of the end of the Pardoner's Tale, to which I referred above, when the Knight reconciles Host and Pardoner, is that the Knight 'is as resistant to critical reflection as the Host, content with conventional assumptions and the established religious institutions'.

In the same way, he asks of the Parson:

> Why should this man feel entitled to make dogmatic utterances about 'soothfastnesse', morality and the sinfulness of other people when he himself must be immersed in the corrupt prison, his vision correspondingly distorted and unreliable? The answer is that he should not. Lacking all self-reflexivity he totally fails to bring the grounds of his discourse, and his own fallen state, into consideration.

I have already suggested that it is hard for us to take the Parson's Tale today. But Aers' arguement convinces me no more than does Jones'. What it seems to me we get in those moments when the pilgrims assent to the Knight or Parson telling his tale is a merging of individuals into a corporate identity, and what I suspect the Parson's Tale is trying to achieve is the presentation of that authoritative voice which is not the voice of Jack or Jill but of an entire community. It is probably true that Chaucer was, like Mozart and unlike Bach or Stravinsky, better at representing the dramatic clash of individual voices than the merging of all into the corporate voice of prayer, but it would be wrong to deny that this is what he was up to.

Aers, of course, would deny it strenuously, because for him the Church, like the State, is an institution, and one so deeply embroiled in the *saeculum* that all pretence to authority is both bogus and oppressive. He sees the medieval ideals of marriage or of the Three Estates as instruments of control by the parties in power, the Church and State, all the more anxious to preserve their privileges as they note the rumblings from below. At one point he quotes Leszek Kolakowski on the difference between the priest and the jester:

> The priest is the guardian of the absolute; he sustains the cult of the

READING THE MIDDLE AGES

final and the obvious as acknowledged by and contained in tradition. The jester is he who moves in good society without belonging to it, and treats it with impertinence; he who doubts all that appears self-evident... to unveil the non-obvious behind the obvious, the non-final behind the final.

Chaucer, of course, is the jester, and Aers warns of 'the disturbing implications of being a jester in a culture where priests and intellectual policemen play a major role'. But Kolakowski's is a deceptive model. England in the Middle Ages was not like Kolakowski's image of communist Russia, and though such remarks have a hard-headed radical ring to them they do nothing to help us understand Chaucer or Langland or their age.

In an earlier and much better book, *Piers Plowman and Christian Allegory* (1975), Aers has argued that the debate among medievalists over whether poets wrote what Erich Auerbach called figural allegory — allegory somehow involved with history and change — or whether they wrote what Aers terms picture allegory — the mere mechanical substitution of one element for another — is not one which can be solved by a simple yes or no. Most medieval theology and literature, he argued, is picture allegory: 'The images are removed from their controlling contexts and attached to certain terms of a different order, pell-mell. Again the time-dimension, so vital to the notion of progressive revelation, is destroyed.' By contrast, Langland is deeply concerned with process, change, the complexities of life. His work is probing and exploratory where that of most poets is static and wooden. 'Once again', he says, 'the critic must stay alert to the process of Landland's figurative modes, and responsive to the particular religious intelligence they manifest.'

I wonder, though, whether the high value we place on terms like 'exploratory', 'probing' and 'process' is not itself historically conditioned. Both Jones and Aers would have us see irony where I suspect there is none. Neither is willing to take something like the description of the Knight or the Tale of the Parson 'straight'; for Aers, to be content, as we are told the Knight and Host are, with 'conventional assumptions and the established religious institutions' is to be not only naïve but party to a monstrous fraud. There is a mighty gap between medieval society as it sees itself and as it 'really' is, and Chaucer and Langland are clear-sighted enough to see through the web of ideology to the reality behind it, while the rest of the literature of the time is content merely to repeat and reinforce it. But this seems to me to be a naïve notion of ideology, and Chaucer and Langland, I suspect, have more in common with their contemporaries than with a poet like Milton, of whom Aers seems (not surprisingly, given the Protestant bent of his mind) to be particularly fond. What, for example, would Aers do with a poem like 'I sing of a Maiden', which seems content to reiterate the commonplaces of the day, yet which is a moving and powerful work of art?

It may be that Aers has not grasped the importance of the lines from Psalm 36 which he quotes from Langland: 'When the just man shall fall, he shall not be bruised: for the Lord putteth his hand under him.' There is a confidence about medieval art which suggests that it all springs from a common ground. This is not easy to analyse, for it is not something to be found 'in' this or that work, but, as I have said, is the common ground from which all spring. That is the significance of *figura*: it is not a technical or poetic *device*, but an expression of the sense of the meaningfulness of history. And it is out of such a sense that Chaucer and Langland question the complex and shifting values of their day.

Scholars bending over individual works are more responsive to the new, the surprising, the individuating, than to the common. Criticism, too, is better equipped for dealing with surface change than with underground continuity. The new volume in Chatto's marvellous series of manuscript illustration is a case in point. The plates, beautifully reproduced, show how close England was to the Continent in the High Middle Ages, and how different the art of the time was from what was to come in the Renaissance. The cover shows what is perhaps the most beautiful painting in the greatest book of the period, the *Très Riches Heures* of the Duc de Berry: Adam and Eve in a circular walled Paradise with a high fountain of life, elaborately wrought, springing up in the centre. The pleasure of the painting, as of all medieval illustration, comes primarily from the assurance with which the design is imposed on the surface of the page. Within the circle of Paradise we are shown four episodes: the Temptation, Eve giving Adam the apple, God accusing them, and the angel sending them out of a magnificent gate which echoes the fountain. The painting is thus a combination of the centred and the decentred. The individual elements, we feel, could not so confidently escape the boundaries of the frame, and move out into the page, were there not a very strong sense of the rightness and necessity of what is being represented. This is a highly sophisticated art, but it partakes of the elements of the most naïve. Indeed, what we term naïvety in medieval art springs from that confidence in a world upheld by God, and it is this which vanishes when the Renaissance encloses paintings firmly within their single frames and single viewpoints — no longer the viewpoint of God, but that of the painter or the viewer.

Yet our art history has for a century or more been dominated by a German, Renaissance-based tradition. Reading Panofsky or Millard Meiss (who has done more than anyone else to make accessible to us the world of art with which this book is concerned), one is easily browbeaten into accepting that Whig view of the history of art which in other fields these brilliantly intelligent scholars would surely be the first to resist. What they focus on is how far such art approximates to the antique and heralds the Renaissance. All that Marcel Thomas can say about the painting of the Garden of Eden, for example, is that Adam in the second episode is clearly modelled on a Roman statue of a wounded Persian. But an unbiased look at the pages reproduced in this volume surely reveals that the whole attitude to the picture is quite different from that of the Italian Renaissance or of Dürer. What we could say of even the most humble medieval manuscript illumination is that its very shortcomings as an aesthetic object are the source of its power, for it conveys, across the centuries, a potent sense of its ground in faith. It is this which led Proust to talk of a little figure almost hidden on a portal of Amiens as striking us with the power, 'not of mere art, but of our deepest memories'.

Proust reminds us that there is an alternative to the German arthistorical tradition. It is the tradition of Ruskin, of Proust himself, of Benjamin on aura, of Adrian Stokes, of Lawrence Gowing on Vermeer. Its patient exploration of the phenomenology of perception, rather than the brilliant and erudite iconographic work of Panofsky and his disciples, can best help us to understand that it is what Chaucer and Langland have in common with the anonymous art of the Middle Ages, not what sets them apart, that is the source of their greatness.

NOTES

*Chaucer's Knight: Portrait of a Medieval Mercenary, Terry Jones, Weidenfeld, £8.95, 1980

Chaucer, Langland and the Creative Imagination, David Aers, Routledge, £9.75, 1980

The Golden Age: Manuscript Painting at the Time of Jean, Duc de Berry, Marcel Thomas, Chatto, £12.50 and £6.95, 1980

1 Ralph Baldwin was, so far as I know, the first to stress this aspect of the poem. See his 'The Unity of the Canterbury Tales', *Anglistica* V. On the 'idea' of the work see Donald Howard's splendid *The Idea of the Canterbury Tales* (1976)

5

A Great Critic *

I have always thought that there was a striking resemblance between Freud's earliest case-histories, which he published as *Studies On Hysteria*, and the Sherlock Holmes stories. In the *Studies*, as in Sherlock Holmes, we are presented with the man of wisdom to whom people bring their problems; who listens in silence; then asks a number of carefully considered questions; and who finally solves the mystery and restores things to the order they were in before tragedy struck — or at least unearths the culprit. There is even an episode in the *Studies* about the great doctor on holiday in a mountain resort. But a man like Freud and Holmes can, of course, never take a holiday: here, too, a mystery is brought to him to solve. Naturally, he obliges.

The clarity and elegance of Freud's accounts cannot hide the enormous amount of sheer knowledge that he brings to each case; that knowledge is never used to impress either the reader or the patient, yet it is there behind every decision and remark the doctor makes. Nor is it simply knowledge about his chosen field: rather, it is an awareness of classical culture, literature and the humanities, which are never seen as mere fields of study but always as part of our lives as civilised human beings.

The same combination of extreme clarity of thought and lightly-carried erudition is to be found in the great German-speaking art historians of this century. Panofsky's essays in particular, like Freud's, convey the excitement of a detective story together with that quite different excitement which comes from seeing great learning deployed for valuable ends. Quite often an essay begins with a particular problem to solve, produces evidence from some learned source which suddenly seems to resolve the difficulties, then points out that this raises a new kind of problem — and so the essay spirals in towards the centre, until not only has the specific question been answered, but the whole of a past epoch has grown meaningful for us.

THE MIRROR OF CRITICISM

Nevertheless, as with Freud, doubts creep in after a while. One senses that behind the apparent catholicity of taste and the seemingly insatiable curiosity about the past, there lies a distinct pattern of prejudices. Gombrich has ably argued that Freud's taste in artistic matters is very much that of the average late nineteenth-century Viennese bourgeois. But what are we to make of Gombrich's own recent remark: 'As one who still likes Beethoven symphonies and is likely to stay away when a modern work is announced...'? Does not the implied opposition smack a little too much of prejudice? Of course, it is possible to see the Warburg school's high valuation of Renaissance and classical art, and its distrust of what seems to be modern irrationality, in historical terms — as its reaction to the Nazi glorification of the primitive — but I think the roots go deeper. Panofsky is really not very far from the average late nineteenth-century Viennese bourgeois when he writes, in his great book on Dürer: 'But where a picture like the woodcut from Colard Mansion's *Ovide Moralisé* of 1484 strikes us as almost comical for want of expressiveness and dramatic concentration, Dürer's drawing, executed only ten years later, has the force of a classic tragedy.' I, on the other hand, find the woodcut utterly delightful, and the Dürer a pompous bore.

Meyer Schapiro is blessedly free of the prejudices of Panofsky and Gombrich. He can, of course, do the classic art-historical thing as well as anyone, but even in the most purely scholarly and erudite essays in this volume his warmth and catholicity shine through. Take the first essay, a study of the symbolism of the Mérode altarpiece, that beautiful late medieval Flemish work now in New York. In a wing beside the Annunciation an aged Joseph is seen in his carpenter's workshop. It seems that he is making a mousetrap. What is the significance of that detail? Schapiro begins by explaining it in terms of the tradition of symbolism which saw Christ as the bait for the Devil, who, in seizing him, brought about his own ruin. This helps to answer our question, but it is clearly not enough. Schapiro notes the importance of the objects in Mary's room in the accompanying picture, remarking that 'the mystery that takes place within the Virgin's body is symbolised in the space of the house; the various objects, all so familiar and tangible... possess a hidden religious meaning, focused on the central human figure.'

The argument now takes a new turn, typical of many of these essays. Schapiro relates the painting not just to an iconographical tradition, but to the history and culture of the time. He quotes Chancellor

A GREAT CRITIC

Gerson's moralised description of Joseph as humble, hard-working and thrifty, and points out the importance of the mousetrap in the painting as a domestic object as well as a theological symbol. This leads him to some very interesting general reflections. In the early Middle Ages the notion that objects in the physical world were an allegory of the spiritual did not necessarily entail the representation of these objects as the signs of hidden truths. 'The mousetrap, like other household objects, had first to be interesting as part of the extended visible world, before its theological significance could justify its presence in a religious picture.' However, even as a piece of still-life, the mousetrap is more than an object in a home: 'it takes its place beside the towel and the basin of water as an instrument of cleanliness or wholeness, and may therefore be regarded as an overt symbol of the Virgin's purity.' What Schapiro is doing here, by stressing the notion of an 'overt symbol', is to open our minds to the possibility that the alternatives are never simply either that objects are symbolic or that they are not: the very way the painter has brought them together makes objects in a naturalistic painting inevitably symbolic.

But Schapiro has not finished. He changes direction again, and reminds us that the picture also shows a beautiful young wife and an old husband busy making mousetraps. We do not need the learned gloss he provides to realise, once it is put like that, that the mousetrap also functions as a sexual symbol. Once again he is concerned to save us from the false alternatives of either a religious meaning or no meaning at all. By presenting the picture in this way, as 'a latent battlefield for the religious conceptions, the new secular values, and the underground wishes of men', he can lead into a superb compressed discussion of the Arnolfini portrait, where the overtly religious content has retreated to the tiny scenes of the life of Christ which encircle the mirror, that 'beautiful, luminous, polished eye', in which the artist himself is caught as he enters the room. And serene though these two great paintings may be, they contain the seeds of the terrifying and fantastic art of Bosch, where the humble mousetrap has turned into those 'ubiquitous Boschian instruments in which the diabolocal, the ingenious and the sinfully erotic are combined'.

Not all the essays are as rich and suggestive as the one on the Mérode altarpiece. However, Schapiro is always alive to the human element, whether he is dealing with Palestinian mosaics or Irish book illumination, with Italian flagellants or the struggle of the native and the Roman Church in the time of Bede. Like any art historian whose field is pre-Renaissance, his sympathy and understanding can never be for the purely aesthetic qualities of objects, for art was always an integral part of life. Discussing the famous Bird's Head Haggada, an illustrated Hebrew manuscript of c.1300, he points out that the book embodies a conception of history and of life: 'Here a people recall their past and affirm a common faith.' The Haggada is not a book for the synagogue but for the assembled family at Seder, and as such it has no counterpart among the service books of medieval Christian ritual. The illustrations may give pleasure to all, but they were never designed to replace the written word, as the stained glass of the churches was supposed to do. 'They were addressed... to the already instructed reader of the text, and re-enacted for his imagination both the historic and the present world referred to in the writing and, like the poetry and song in the same book, helped to save him from a merely intellectual grasp of a content steeped in feeling as well as thought.'

Though Schapiro rarely spends much time on general remarks, no reader of his work can fail to realise that he is, in his modest and quiet way, profoundly altering our views of the past. Like Peter Brown in his studies of late antiquity, he helps to free us from a Rome-centred view of the past, and allows us to recognise that the eastern Mediterranean was the source of western culture, and that the art of Ireland, Spain and Norway is as important for us as that of Italy or France. The Israeli poet, Yehuda Amichai, was making the same point when, in a recent interview with Tony Rudolf, he stressed the kinship he felt with such poets as Seferis and Montale: for too long our geography and our history have made us look at things in the wrong way, and by doing so they have cut us off from an important part of ourselves. It is not just today that English painters are among the most highly respected in the world; the great age of English art was around the year 1000, and a number of the essays in this book analyse the extraordinary flowering of English art in the late Anglo-Saxon period, and its relations with Byzantine and Romanesque art.

Every art historian must be able to describe in words the works with which he is dealing, but Schapiro's gifts are quite outstanding. Here he is writing about mosaic pavements in Israel:

> No part of the surface is, strictly speaking, a neutral ground. From this uniformity of the tiny elements arise a typical texture and rhythm and a scale of proportion of parts to the whole. Many objects — a petal, an eye, a nostril — are represented by a single

cube which becomes a measure throughout. By their equal density and common structure the cubes and joints help to unify an extended horizontal field which we cannot easily see as a whole but must grasp through successive views as we move around it. Important, too, are the characteristic hardness and opacity of the slightly lustrous medium with its considerable range of stony and earthen tones; with the grayness of the joints they confer an aspect of the sober and subdued, a humble materiality that distinguishes the floor mosaics from the more colourful and luminous glass mosaics on the walls and vaults.

After such a description, which is itself already a response to what is before him, Schapiro has no difficulty in showing that the marvellous mosaic of the sacrifice of Isaac, if it owes nothing to classical models, is very far from being 'primitive' either. Like the work of Paul Zumthor in the field of medieval literature, Schapiro's essays help us to see the inadequacy of notions of artistic norms derived from the Renaissance. 'The standard of nature is an obstacle to critical insight,' he remarks at one point in his characteristically quiet tone, and he proceeds to demonstrate the truth of this in his analyses of the extraordinary exuberance of medieval English art or of the wonderful Beatus apocalypse from Spain.[1] 'The Beatus manuscripts', he says, 'make us realise how limited is our present conception of the artistic process, and how much it depends on the values of art and social life today.' He goes on:

> we are able, however, precisely through our own art and point of view, to appreciate these long-ignored medieval works as few observers could do during the last centuries before our time.
> ... I do not think that I am fanciful in seeing in certain of Léger's works, painted during his stay in New York in the 1940s, the effects of his enthisiasm for this Spanish manuscript.

Schapiro is right not to try to be polemical.[2] It is enough that we recognise that the great artists of the present have helped us to see what we had for so long been blind to. Pierre Daix's exciting recent book on Picasso's Cubist years makes the point repeatedly: to go forward, one has to go back, just as to be able to go back one has to go forward. And it is not simply a matter of art and art history. The uncanny sympathy with animals exhibited by Kafka is something which others have perhaps felt, though few can have felt it as strongly, but which culture somehow didn't allow them to articulate.

THE MIRROR OF CRITICISM

It was of Kafka that I particularly thought as I read what is perhaps the finest essay in this book, a mere two-page review of Lilian Randall's *Images in the Margins of Gothic Manuscripts*. 'Though scattered capriciously in the margins,' says Schapiro,

> they are done with the same precision of detail and calligraphic finesse as the richly framed religious imagery on the same page. They are a convincing evidence of the artist's liberty, his unconstrained possession of the space, which confounds the view of medieval art as a model of systematic order and piety. There is also in these images a sweetness and charm which seem to arise from the truly miniature scale — a scale that is not just a consequence of the small format of the book made for private reading and prayer; it is a quality of the objects represented.

Only a writer with his eye firmly on the object and the expressive ability to convey what he sees could nowadays risk a phrase like 'sweetness and charm'. But Schapiro, one feels, always knows what he is doing, always says what he means, and he has first-hand experience of such a wide range of art that his analogies are always illuminating. Here, for example, he goes on to suggest that for sureness of touch in their depiction of hares, apes, mice, cats, birds, snails, insects and flowers these painters are equalled only by their contemporaries in the Far East.

But this is not all. By reducing man to the scale of these creatures, by

> a hybrid mingling of bodies which form together an undemountable dwarf, a monstricule, the artist strips man of his privilege and supremacy; we see him in these strange re-embodiments as a being among the others in nature, and sharing in his movements and passions the instinctive mobility of the animal world. ... It is a process of desublimation through which the distance between the natural and the civilised is abolished. No other art in history offers so abundant an imagery of the naked and clothed body as a physical engine. Free from classic norms, the artist experiments with the human frame as the most flexible, ductile, indefatigably protean self-deforming system in nature.

This is art history at its best, a truly humanistic activity, since it helps to give man back to himself and his possibilities, both by pointing out what lay before our eyes but which we had missed seeing for so long, and by its own inimitable example.

A GREAT CRITIC

NOTES

Late Antique, Early Christian and Medieval Art: Selected Papers, Vol. 3, Meyer Schapiro, Chatto & Windus, £20, 1980

1 It is a great pity that this otherwise beautifully produced book does not run to coloured illustrations. A good deal of Schapiro's analysis of the Beatus apocalypse will thus be lost on the reader, since that work depends to a large extent on the strikingly bold colouring. But he can make up for it by purchasing another Chatto volume in their series of manuscript illuminations, *Early Spanish Manuscript Illumination*, by John Williams.

2 His remarks here need to be filled out by reading his superb essays on Van Gogh, Picasso and Mondrian in *Selected Papers*, Vol. II, *Modern Art*.

6

Rabelais and the Role of Fiction*

The moments in the history of art when a door is suddenly opened onto a wholly new range of possibilities are extremely rare. Monteverdi's *Orfeo* marks one such in the history of music; Cézanne's late canvases another, in the history of painting. The works of Rabelais, beginning with *Pantagruel*, first published in Lyons in 1532, most definitely mark one in the history of literature.

Historians and scholars are much concerned with origins, precursors, and influences. But when one is faced with something wholly new such considerations can blunt rather than sharpen one's responses. Is it possible to put oneself in the position of the first reader of *Pantagruel*? To try to recapture the sense of exhilaration and bafflement that always accompanies confrontation with that which is totally new in art? Such readers would have known that a chapbook had recently appeared, called *Les Grandes et inestimables cronicques du grant et enorme geant Gargantua*, and that it had been a wildfire success. They would pick up Pantagruel expecting more of the same, for the sub-title explicitly tells us that this is 'Son of Gargantua' — *Les Horribles et espouventables faicts et prouesses du tresrenommé Pantagruel, Roi des Dipsodes, fils du grand geant Gargantua*. But here, after a brief prologue, is what they would find:

> It will not be an idle nor an unprofitable thing, seeing we are at leisure, to put you in minde of the Fountain and Original Source, whence is derived unto us the good Pantagruel; for I see that all good Historiographers have thus handled their Chronicle: not only Arabians, Barbarians and Latines, but also the gentle Greeks, who were eternal drinkers. You must therefore remark, that at the beginning of the world, (I speak of a long time, it is above fourty nights, according to the supputation of the ancient Druids) a little

after that Abel was killed by his brother Cain, the earth, imbrued with that blood of the just, was one year so exceeding fertile in all those fruits which it usually produceth to us, and especially in Medlars, that ever since, throughout all the ages, it hath been called the years of the great medlars.[1]

We are present here at nothing less than the birth of the novel. An important moment (though hardly a solemn one), and one we would do well to try to understand. Three aspects of the passage call for comment: the insistence on origins; the invocation of authorities; and the tone.

No medieval story is much concerned with tracing things back to their sources. Either it's 'once upon a time' ('whilom'), or it's *when* or *after* this or that happened ('after that the siege and the assault was ceased at Troy'); other narratives begin with the poet falling asleep or coming to in a dark wood, where the landscape tells us what tradition and what traditional images the poet is evoking. Just as few medieval churches can really be said to date from this or that time, since there had always been a church or shrine on the spot, so no medieval story can be said to be original or new. But this story is different. Rabelais — or Alcofribas Nasier, as he anagramatically calls himself on the title page — wants to put us 'in minde of the Fountain and Original Source, whence is derived unto us the good Pantagruel...'. One of the elements of the novel as it develops in the eighteenth century is going to be this insistence on birth, the single source, uniqueness, novelty.

The narrator, however, is equally anxious to assure us of the truth and historicity of his tale: 'A little after that Abel was killed by his brother Cain...'. No assertion, however trivial, is allowed to slip by without reinforcement from a venerable authority: 'according to the supputation of the ancient Druids...'. Truth, authenticity, thus joins originality as an essential element in the birth of the new form.

But the most significant element in the passage is also the most difficult to pin down: it resides in the *tone*. No reader can fail to realise, after a line or two, that all is not as it should be with this narrative. There is a growing sense of disparity between *what* is said, and *how* it is being said. By the time we get to the medlars we need to go back and reread the paragraph. When we do so we are struck by the little aside about the gentle Greeks, a phrase we had no doubt ignored at a first reading as it seemed out of keeping with the effect of the weightiness of authority the narrator seemed to want to convey, but which now is seen as holding the true key to the tone. In other words the lack of interest and importance, the lack even of any reality of 'the good Pantagruel', is borne in upon us precisely by the impressive array of stylistic and rhetorical gestures which herald him.

But we misread the passage if we conclude from this that Rabelais is being ironic at the expense of the giant. The disparity between style and content contaminates both historical truth and fabulous narrative. Looking back once again at the passage we note that it addresses itself to a 'we' who include both author and readers, and who are said to be 'at leisure'. This leisure, this hiatus in the busy day, is the space where narrative inserts itself. Later Rabelais — like Nashe and Sterne — will say that he threw off the book while eating and drinking. The scholar, seeing the brilliance of the work, will want to dismiss such a remark, but we ought perhaps to take it seriously. In contrast to the medieval poet, who has a vision to impart or a tale to narrate to a community of men who share the same assumptions and interests as himself, Alcofribas Nasier talks merely to pass the time, and he addresses himself to the solitary reader who, like himself, has leisure on his hands.

For Rabelais, in 1532, two options were open: he could go on writing commentaries on ancient authorities, like the ones on Galen and Hippocrates he was called upon to undertake in the course of his medical studies; or he could write merry tales in the vernacular, as Boccaccio had done, or as, more recently, the author of the *Grands Croniques* had done with notable success. He was condemned, in other words, either to gloss The Truth, or to spin lies out of his own entrails. He chose, of course, to do neither, but to explore instead his own unease with both.[2] In other words, he chose to use the impulse to write as a way of discovering where lay his subject matter: he chose the extemporal vein.

The birth of the novel is coterminous with the birth of the extemporal vein. No one, least of all the author, could have predicted those medlars at the start of his story, but here they are making an appearance and we are not yet two sentences into the chapter. They appear not because Rabelais wants to make a point or create a character, but simply because the logic of his discourse has brought him here. The only question that now faces him is: Where does one go from here?

The reader too is launched into the unknown, all the normal props whipped away from under him. The timid reader will quickly shut the

RABELAIS AND THE ROLE OF FICTION

book and look for something safer; the more intrepid reader will cling on and gradually grow to relish the danger. But even he may not quite see where the newness of the extemporal style really lies.

All art is the result of exclusion. The systems of exclusion of art are its forms: the sonnet, the elegy, the five act tragedy. Thus there will always be a gap between the impulse toward expression, which is chaotic and limitless, and its embodiment in the forms of art — a dark area where the crucial transformation takes place and which, it seems, must always remain shrouded. This is where the novelty of the novel lies. For suddenly it seems that everything can be said, that our doubts and hesitations, the gaps in memory and desire, the inevitable and repeated failures to turn chaos into form, to make sense of past and present — all this can now be given expression, can have conferred upon it the dignity of art, need no longer be a source of shame.

Thus to refer to *Pantagruel* as a Menippean satire, to relate it, as scholars have done, to Erasmus's *Praise of Folly* or Brant's *Ship of Fools*, is to miss the central point. Those works do indeed exist in a particular tradition, a distinctive genre. To write in that tradition is to make a pact with your reader beforehand: this is the kind of work it's going to be. With *Pantagruel* the only sign to the reader is a warning: hold on tight.

But of course rules sustain at the same time as they exclude — whether in the sonnet or the five act tragedy. Very soon the novel too, out of a natural spirit of self-preservation, started to build up its own tacit rules: rules regulating the tense of the narrative, the degree of authorial intervention, the way character is to be presented, etc. The nineteenth-century-novel is as tight a genre as the sonnet, though, unlike the sonnet, it conceals the fact — sometimes even from its own practitioners. Only a handful of authors in the long history of the novel have managed to keep open the door unlocked by Rabelais: Cervantes, Fielding perhaps, Sterne. It was not until this century that a new desire was to manifest itself on the part of a wide range of writers to return to the freedom of the extemporal vein.

The extemporalist trusts to the moment: it will provide. In the case of most writers it doesn't. It would have been much better for them, we feel, to have accepted the constraints of the traditional novel. We, as readers, grow restive as the outlines of the writer's self start to emerge, as his own private obsessions grow more and more blatant. The exclusions of art, its forms, have the function of directing the writer to what is most valuable and interesting, putting him in touch with the experience of all earlier practitioners of the genre. Without them he is usually only a bore.

How does Rabelais escape these strictures? Partly, he was lucky. He happened to be writing at the right time. Partly too, like Sterne and Proust and Kafka, he combined immense patience with immense reserves, cultural, linguistic, and human.

Is Rabelais merely, as Donald Frame suggests, 'intoxicated with words', never using two when six or even sixty will do? Here is part of a passage from the Prologue to the Third Book, where sixty-four verbs in the imperfect tense are used to describe how Diogenes drove his barrel out of the city of Corinth and up and down a nearby mountain:

> le tournoit, viroit, brouilloit, garbouilloit, hersoit, versoit, renversoit, nattoit, grattoit, flattoit, barattoit, bastoit, boutoit, butoit, tabustoit, cullebutoit, trepoit, trempoit, tapoit...

Frame correctly observes that 'what is apparent is how one sound leads to another similar one', but he fails to do anything with this insight. Yet what we see at work here is a continuous to-and-fro motion between the word as pure object, sheer breath, and the word as part of a system of signs conveying meaning.

This is typical of Rabelais's tactic throughout: he leads us to the point where the realistic surface, his story of giants and battles, the education of gentlemen and the acquiring of wives, is just about to burst and disintegrate, and then pulls us back to the narrative and carries on. We can see this at work again in the marvellous description of Gargantua's youthful games. (*Gargantua*, ch. 11). 'Gargantua', Rabelais begins by telling us, 'from three years upwards unto five, was brought up and instructed in all convenient discipline, by the commandment of his father.' However, naturally enough, he 'spent that time like the other little children of the countrey, that is, in drinking, eating and sleeping.'

So far this could be the description of any fictional childhood; but at this point the chapter ceases merely to convey information, and starts instead to mime the young giant's activity: 'that is, in drinking, eating and sleeping; in eating, sleeping and drinking; and in sleeping, drinking and eating'. Now the narrative beings to go wild:

> Still he wallowed and rowled up and down himself in the mire and dirt: he blurred and sullied his nose with filth: he blotted and smutch't his face with any kinds of scurvie stuffe, he trode down his

shoes in the heele: At the flies he did oftentimes yawn, and ran very heartily after the Butterflies...

This change of direction is the signal for the introduction of a seemingly endless series of actions attributed to the young Gargantua, actions which grow more and more preposterous, for what Rabelais does is to take literally a wide range of popular proverbs and locutions. Thus

> he would sit down betwixt two stooles, and his arse to the ground, would cover himself with a wet sack, and drinke in eating of his soupe.... He would flay the Fox, say the Apes Paternoster, return to his sheep and turn the Hogs to the Hay.... He always looked a given horse in the mouth, leaped from the cock to the asse, and put one ripe between two green: by robbing Peter he payed Paul, he kept the Moon from the wolves, and hoped to catch Larks if ever the Heavens should fall....'

This amazing sequence modulates gradually into a lyrical passage about the sexual games played by the young Gargantua with his nurses and then into a wonderful chorus by the nurses in praise of his sexual organ: 'One of them would call it her little dille, her staffe of love, her quillety, her faucetin, her dandilollie: Another her peen, her jolly kyle...'. Whereupon the narrative finally returns to its task at the start of the following chapter, with the reintroduction of time: 'Afterwards, that he might be all his lifetime a good Rider, they made to him a fair great horse of wood...'

As we can see from this passage, Rabelais moves continually, yo-yo fashion, between the pleasure and reality principles, between the expression of the unlimited desires of the child and the reminder of the limits imposed by the external world: sexual taboos, the laws of grammar and syntax. The whole of this book is thus rather like Wagner's *Tristan*: a perpetually deferred climax which, if it were allowed to take place, would destroy the work.

Rabelais, then, is not primarily interested in character or plot. Compare, for example, the attitudes of Rabelais and Cervantes to the popular tales from which they take off. Rabelais *retells* the tale, while Cervantes creates a character who *lives* the tales. The English — is it because of Shakespeare? — have always responded better to solutions of the latter kind. Even Joyce, whose instinct was to go in the direction of Rabelais, felt compelled to create 'characters'; and it is Beckett's lack of interest in character that makes him so difficult to read for anyone brought up in the English literary tradition.

Rabelais provides himself with just enough character and plot to keep going — a few names, a few simple oppositions: Pantagruel-Panurge, Baisecul-Humevesne; some large, loose, episodic structures: wars, quests, symposia. His way forward from episode to episode, chapter to chapter, does not rely on these. What he does instead is to let all the voices inside him and inside his culture have their head. He echoes the multiplicity of languages available to him: not just the many modern and ancient languages of which the Renaissance was becoming aware, but the language of the law courts, of the marketplace, of commerce, of Humanist letters, of diplomacy, historiography, rhetorical praise and rhetorical lament. He inserts himself into each of these, draws his sustenance from it, and allows each to overreach itself just enough to give us a glimpse of what he is doing. We have seen this at work in the opening sentences of *Pantagruel*, but it is true even of the famous Humanist documents such as the letters of the giants, or the harangues of Janotus de Bragmardo and Ulrich Gallet. Listen to Ambassador Gallet begin his speech:

> There cannot arise amongst men a juster cause of grief, then when they receive hurt and damage, where they may justly expect for favour and good will; and not without cause, (though without reason), have many, after they had fallen into such a calamitous accident, esteemed this indignity lesse supportable then the losse of their own lives, in such sort, that if they have not been able...

The slightly over-insistent Ciceronianisms here draw attention to themselves, allowing us to glimpse the playful artist behind the solemn speaker.

The difference between writing like this and writing within the conventions of the traditional novel is rather like the difference between the stand-up comic and the actor in Ibsen or Chekhov. For the comic there is no safety. No wonder that the incompetent comic gets frightened, talks too much, too fast, dries up, loses the thread, looks round wildly for the exit. The master comic, on the other hand, takes his time, plays the audience. Our pleasure derives not from what he says or does, but from the combination of extreme vulnerability — he's out there, all alone, with no script and no one to help him — and extreme control. In that situation he presents us with a true image of ourselves out in the wide world, and we realise, watching him, how *un*realistic the plays of Ibsen and Chekhov in fact are.

Of course the writer in the extemporal style is less vulnerable than the stand-up comic. He is free, after all, to stop and start again. But the act of writing can also take him much further into the unexpected and unknown than the comic would care to go. The initial encounter between Pantagruel and Panurge is instructive here. In a courteous and flowery French the young prince questions the handsome but ragged Panurge who appears before him: Who are you? he asks. Where do you come from? What is your name? Panurge replies, equally courteously, first in Dutch, then in nonsense jargon, then in Italian, English, Basque, Spanish, Danish, Hebrew, Greek, and Latin. 'Well, my friend,' says Pantagruel, 'but cannot you speak in French?' 'That I can do, Sir, very well,' answers Panurge, 'God be thanked; it is my natural language and mother-tongue.'

Although Pantagruel is held up as an ideal throughout the book, and Panurge is shown to be vain, egotistical, and blind to his innumerable faults, the book, strangely enough, seems rather to be written by a Panurge than by a Pantagruel. But this is not altogether surprising. Like Panurge, the writer of the book has no name, comes from nowhere, and has no tradition to tell him how to speak or what to say. All he has are his wits and his impulse to imitate or mime everything he sees and hears. Sensing himself excluded from the societies of men he can only draw attention to this exclusion by borrowing the diverse tongues and gestures of men. Panurge's surprising mode of reply makes us see that Pantagruel's initial questions were couched in a *certain* language, a single, closed system; for Pantagruel it was the only one and perfectly natural. Panurge will not accept the tacit rules of any society; his language is French, but he will speak it only when asked point-blank if he can do so; otherwise he might as well speak in any of the multiplicity of languages which come just as easily to him. Panurge's reply, however, not only makes us see the limits of Pantagruel's world; there is also something excessive about it, as though the very ease of Pantagruel's use of language had thrown him into a frenzy. We feel in Panurge a positive urge toward dispersal and fragmentation. it is this urge and the way it is just held in check that gives us Rabelais' characteristic tone.

The medieval artist was a craftsman, experienced and adept at his trade; his subject matter was given him by tradition and his job was to rework it in his own way. For this the Renaissance substituted a new image, that of the artist as truth-teller and seer, rising above the muddled world of men and in touch with the mysteries of the universe.[3] Rabelais could not subscribe to this view. He is no prophet and he is aware of the presumptions of pretending to be one. On the other hand, though he retains a sense of the craftsman's cunning and instinct, he senses too that he is now on his own, no longer part of any tradition which can support him. In Rabelais, for the first time, we find the urge to speak allied to the awareness that he has nothing to say. Accepting the challenge, he fragments and disperses himself to the four winds and, in the process of following his nose, his pen, he finds himself again, not an impersonal 'maker', and not the wise Doctor François Rabelais, but anagramatised into Alcofribas Nasier, the eternal trickster, cocking a snook at our solemnities. His 'natural language and mother-tongue', the gift of the vernacular, is the sign of his (and our) exclusion from tradition, but it is also the sign of his (and our) freedom to move among all languages and to remain confined to none. It is the glory and the despair of the novel.

Pantagruel was published in 1532. By 1553 Rabelais was dead. In those twenty years he published three more volumes of his 'novel', and a fifth volume, written at least in part by him, appeared after his death. But already by 1549 the door he had opened had started to be pushed shut. In that year du Bellay published his *Defense et illustration de la langue française*, a key document, as everyone knows, in the cultural history of France. What du Bellay did in that essay was to glorify the vernacular by conferring upon it the status of Latin. The result was to turn the vernacular into yet another closed system, as rigidly exclusive as any poetic language. Extraordinarily enough, it was not until Proust and, after him, Céline and Queneau, that French literature was able to escape the tyranny of Humanist ideals and rediscover the openness and fluidity of Rabelais. (The whole history of nineteenth-century French literature from Châteaubriand to Rimbaud can be seen as the history of futile attempts at revolt, futile because revolt itself was still seen in the terms imposed by the dominant culture.)

It is therefore not surprising that French scholars have tended to see Rabelais exclusively in Humanist terms, and have been quite unable to see the nature of his originality and importance. English scholars, however, should have known better. After all, our great Renaissance writers are not only Spenser and Milton but Shakespeare, Jonson, Nashe, and Donne. England escaped the establishment of a literary academy and the line of Shakespeare and Donne stretched on through

RABELAIS AND THE ROLE OF FICTION

the high age of the Augustans in such writers as Swift, Fielding and Sterne.

But of course scholars, whether English or French, have a vested interest in Humanist ideals. Scholarship needs to sort out, pin down, classify, *understand*. Is it surprising that it has failed to deal with Rabelais? This is not to say that scholarship has not taught us a great deal about the background to Rabelais. It has also used Rabelais extensively in its study of numerous facets of the Renaissance. But when it comes to what is really important about Rabelais, scholarship is not only silent, it is misleading.

Donald Frame's book is a good example of what I mean. Frame is a learned man, the author of several books on Montaigne. He obviously loves and admires Rabelais, and he is both sensitive and commonsensical, surely a good combination in any critic. 'In most writers', he points out, and his tone invites assent, 'the comic touch cancels a serious part that precedes it, puts that too in a comic light. This, I think, is not Rabelais's intent, nor is it his effect on most readers. Neither voice cancels out the other; both continue to sound in our inward ear. Ours to harmonize them as best we can; for the book includes them both.'

Frame sets about analysing Rabelais's book in a detached, scientific spirit. He divides his own book into seventeen chapters: the first deals with the background; the second with the life; the next five with each of Rabelais's five books; and the last ten with a variety of topics from comedy and satire to obscenity and story telling. In each of the chapters dealing with the individual books he goes about things in the same spirit: the book is divided and sub-divided so that we can get a clear idea of what it is about. Thus for *Pantagruel*: 'The book as a whole may be divided into three parts: genealogy, birth, childhood episodes (chapters 1-8); Panurge (9-24); the war and what follows (25-34).' And for *Gargantua*: 'The fifty-eight chapters ... may be divided as follows: 1-13, genealogy, birth, childhood; 14-15 and 21-24, education; 16-20, arrival in Paris...; 25-51, the war against... Picrochole; 52-57, the Abbey of Theleme; 58, the prophetic enigma.'

Frame now proceeds to comment on this analysis: 'Even this outline shows that twelve chapters (as against one plus of *Pantagruel*) are devoted to serious ideas.' At this point we begin to see how Frame's assumptions colour his understanding. For him, despite his opening disclaimer, the book is made up of separate portions of 'light' and of 'serious' material, and Rabelais is given more marks the greater the proportion of 'serious' to 'light' in any book.

At one go this sweeps away any hope of understanding what is distinctive and important in Rabelais' narrative. Indeed, the fact that this is a story and not an encyclopedia is not noticed at all, except for the ritual-like assertion that 'storytelling is one of Rabelais's greatest gifts'. For Frame the narrative is merely a repository of ideas, and those ideas are the ones held by François Rabelais. 'Of all five books,' we are told, '*Gargantua* gives the clearest picture of Rabelais's attitudes and ideas — those of around 1534.'

Frame's assumptions, we begin to see, impose a profoundly misleading reading on the whole book, 'It is no wonder', he remarks, 'that the exuberant optimism of Rabelais's first two books... written before the Placards, is absent from the last three.' However, 'his book was new, his own, and an immediate hit.' Later, though, he qualifies this: 'In his first venture into this form Rabelais is not yet ready to make it his own... He seems to feel limited by the genre in which he chose to write.' Like other scholars, Frame is naturally puzzled why Rabelais should have chosen to write the way he did if what he wanted to do was to discourse on the glorious new dawn of the Renaissance: 'It was a venture that might bring him not only general popularity but also the scorn of other humanists.... Probably Rabelais needed the money.' No doubt he did; writers usually do. But the remark cannot disguise the critical bankruptcy of 'scholarship' when faced with the text of Rabelais. It really comes as no surprise after this to be told that 'much of the plot is episodic'; that 'there are inconsistencies'; and that 'as a literary creation' Panurge 'remains in this book not yet fully a man of flesh and blood but somewhat two-dimensional'.

There is a ghost hovering behind Frame's book — or rather, a ghostly model of what human beings are like and of what art is for. We can reconstitute it quite easily: a man stands clearly defined, over against the world; has inside him certain ideas or views which he wants to convey; these ideas have to do either with the outside world or with the world inside the man; and he writes in order to convey them to the reader, who takes them off the page, so to speak, and places them inside *his* self. This is a model, fostered by Humanism itself, whose power and fascination Rabelais instinctively understood and wished to mock and exorcise. For Humanists it is axiomatic that a text (or a person), cleansed of the accretions of false traditions, can and will speak for itself; that if there is a mystery, it will be solved; that for every riddle there is an answer; and that when that answer is found all the doubts, hesitations, and anxieties of our present existence will be resolved once and for all. Rabelais was more modest in his expectations, and for that reason ultimately more optimistic. He knew that ancient texts, however well edited, still need to be interpreted; he knew, like Hamlet, that it is not possible to pluck out the heart of any man's mystery and that men are no easier to be played on than pipes; he knew that there is no Grail or final goal which will lead to Utopia here on earth; and he knew, finally, that we cannot return to 'the Fountain and Original source' of our own or any other story. However, 'seeing we are at leisure', we can explore this very human though misguided impulse to find truth at all costs, to explain and understand *everything*. If we care to read him, with concentration though without undue seriousness, we shall find that we do indeed make a number of discoveries, but that they are in the main discoveries about our own shortcomings and our own potential: about how frightening and exhilarating it is to cease to be François Rabelais and to become instead Alcofribas Nasier *abstracteur de quinte essence*.

NOTES

*François Rabelais: A Study, Donald Frame, Harcourt Brace Jovanovich, $12.95

1 The translation I use here is that of Sir Thomas Urquhart, published in 1653. Despite its inevitable shortcomings it still seems to me to catch Rabelais's tone better than any other.
2 The point is well made by Michel Beaujour in what is undoubtedly the finest book on Rabelais: *Le Jeu de Rabelais* (Paris, L'Herne, 1969).
3 The Humanist over evaluation of the seer at the expense of the craftsman merely repeats Plato's rejection of *metis* in favour of *logos*. So great was the power and influence of the Platonic dispensation that the enormous range and subtlety of Greek thinking about *metis*, craftsmanly skill and cunning, was more or less repressed from the European consciousness. Marcel Detienne and Jean-Pierre Vernant, in *Les Ruses de l'intelligence: le mètis des grecs* (Paris, Flammarion, 1974), have done much to bring this aspect of Greek culture to life again for us, and what they have to say is profoundly relevant to any attempt to understand the extemporal style and the incomprehension with which it has largely been met. An English translation has been published by the Harvester Press, *Cunning Intelligence in Greek Culture and Society*.

7

A Life and a Half*

Not much is known about Cervantes. He was born in 1547 in Alcalá de Henares, not far from Madrid. His grandfather, a specialist in fiscal law for the Inquisition, had amassed a fortune by shady means, and then withdrawn to another city with a former mistress, leaving his children, to whom he had given no proper education, to fend for themselves. The burden of looking after the family fell on Roderigo, Cervantes' father, who had the unfortunate idea of becoming a surgeon to support his dependants. At the time it was doctors, with their university degrees, who achieved fame and wealth, leaving to ill-paid and ill-trained surgeons the mundane tasks of splinting broken limbs, administering purges and bleeding for the fever. To avoid the constant threat of having their goods confiscated or being thrown into prison for debt, the family was always on the move: Valladolid (the Court city), Córdoba, Seville, finally Madrid.

In such an atmosphere, naturally enough, Cervantes received little formal schooling, though in Madrid he seems to have come under the influence of an Erasmian schoolmaster, who encouraged his first efforts at writing poetry. A sonnet he wrote at the age of twenty to celebrate the birth of the Queen's second daughter has come down to us: it is not a good poem. By 1569, however, Cervantes was in Italy, in the household of a wealthy patron, and the following year he and his brother enlisted, both of them taking part in the Battle of Lepanto in 1571 — Cervantes was wounded three times, and even had his left hand shot off. In 1575, while still a soldier with the fleet, he was captured by a Corsair ship and taken as a slave to Algiers. After four abortive escape attempts he was finally ransomed in 1580.

By this time he was writing (unsuccessful) plays, as well as poems, and in 1585 published a pastoral novel, *La Galatea*. The previous year he had fathered a daughter and married not the mother, but a small-

A LIFE AND A HALF

town girl, eighteen years his junior. No sooner was he married, however, than he was off on his travels again, and for the next twenty years we find him trying to scrape a living, first commandeering provisions for the Armada, then as tax-collector. In both jobs he seems to have been ground between the nether millstone of wily peasants and the upper millstone of crooked bureaucrats, and we hear of him in constant trouble, and even in jail for a crime he almost certainly did not commit. He must, however, have been writing, for *Don Quixote* Part I was published in 1605 and was an immediate success. By this time Cervantes was back with his wife, sisters and their dependants, living in Valladolid. The fame of his novel brought him little financial reward, but now he was writing in earnest, and in 1613 published the *Exemplary Tales*, followed by the *Voyage to Parnassus* in 1614, *Don Quixote*, Part II in 1615, and *Persiles and Sigismunda*, the unreadable epic romance he was sure would seal his reputation, in 1617. He was not alive when it was published: he died on the same day as Shakespeare, in 1616.

Such, in brief, are the facts about the author of *Don Quixote*. Like most men and women before the seventeenth century, he has left us no letters, no diaries, none of that wealth of material which makes the life of a Keats or a Kafka so enthralling. The biographer only has the dry documents to go on: Court records, petitions, bills. Sometimes, it is true, the documents are not so dry. In 1509, for example, Cervantes' sister submitted a petition to the Council of the Indies, which is a little biography in itself:

> Miguel de Cervantes Saavedra says he has served Your Majesty many years in the campaigns on sea and land which have occurred in the past twenty-two years, especially in the Naval Battle, in which he received many wounds, including the loss of a hand from a harquebus ball. And the following year he was at Navarino and later in action at Tunis and La Goleta. And *en route* to this Court with letters from my lord Don Juan and from the Duke of Sessa so that Your Majesty might show him favour he was captured in the galley *Sol*, he and his brother, who also served Your Majesty in the same campaigns, and they were taken to Algiers, where they spent such heritage as they had in ransoming themselves, along with their parents' whole estate and the dowries of two maiden sisters, who were impoverished through ransoming their brothers. And after their liberation, they served Your Majesty in the Kingdom of

THE MIRROR OF CRITICISM

Portugal and in the Terceiras [Azores] with the Marquis of Santa Cruz.... And in all that time no favour has been granted him. He requests and beseeches as humbly as he can that Your Majesty be pleased to favour him with a post in the Indies... for he will fulfil any of those offices Your Majesty might grant him because he is an able and competent man and deserving of Your Majesty's favour and because his wish is to continue to serve Your Majesty always and to end his life as his forebears have, for in it he will receive great favour and reward.

Scribbled above Cervantes' signature is a notation by a Council member: 'Let him look closer to home for such favour as may be granted him.'

This is chilling. But most often of course the records are not only dull but difficult to interpret. 'Do the two documents refer to the same Miguel de Cervantes?' asks Byron at one point. 'Probably they do,' he replies; but we are left to wonder. Elsewhere he remarks disarmingly: 'What was Cervantes up to while plague, famine, corruption and literary gloom swirled round him? It depends on which biographer you read. The documentary gaps are wide enough to drive armies of theories through.'

In such a situation the would-be biographer is driven back on that favourite device — 'filling in the background'. With a writer separated from us by four centuries, and who is the product of a culture few readers of *Don Quixote* are likely to be familiar with, this is no bad thing. Byron is quite good at sketching in the social, political and intellectual scene. He rightly stresses the crucial importance of the Reconquest, completed in 1492, when the Moors were finally driven from Granada, where they had been living for eight centuries. For Spain in the Middle Ages had accommodated Jews, Moors and Christians in extraordinary harmony. But by the end of the fifteenth century a new spirit of intransigence had set in. Spain was now a military Christian country, and Moors and Jews had been forced to flee or to convert. The consequences of this were enormous: not only are some of the greatest figures of the sixteenth century (most probably including Cervantes himself) *conversos*, but the atmosphere of chauvinism and xenophobia had a profound effect on intellectual life. As the triumphs of the early years gave way to the agonies of the war with Holland and then the ignominious defeat of the Armada, there was a growing rift between the complex and confused social realities and the oversimplified ideals of honour that continued, more and more obsessively, to be voiced. It is not surprising that by the turn of the century the Spaniard was regularly appearing in other European literatures as a figure of fun, an absurd posturing ninny whom it was impossible to take seriously. Yet this was also the golden age of Spanish literature, the century of St John of the Cross, Lope, Quevedo, Góngora.

Byron has read widely in the secondary literature, and he deftly captures the multiple contradictions. He is also good at the set-pieces, such as the Battle of Lepanto or the horrors of an Algerian jail. As one reads on, however, one begins to wonder whether this kind of narrative history really advances our understanding. One longs for the timeless history of a Braudel or the sharp focus on a single year, a single event, of a Le Roy Ladurie. Instead, Byron only goes once more over ground covered in countless traditional history books. He also has the unfortunate vice of the popular biographer and historical novelist, which is best illustrated by a quotation:

> Well, the golden halls were there; so were the marble libraries and the paintings. He could see them, perhaps, as he trotted in his master's velvet-sheathed shadow at the Vatican, or wandered the city alone in those few hours when Acquaviva had no need of him. There were plenty of people in Rome he might have liked to meet. El Greco was there then.

By the end of the book we are not merely uneasy with this particular enterprise, but with the whole nature of the genre Byron has chosen. Ours, it is true, is an age of biography. The two-volume Lives pour off the presses, snatch up the leading reviews, and no doubt sell in their thousands. My feelings about this phenomenon are mixed. It is true that the more information one has about an artist one admires the better. Deirdre Bair's biography of Beckett was a case in point: one was glad of the information, the quotes from the letters, even if the writing was not very distinguished. On the other hand, the hunger for biographical facts about writers who have just died or are even still alive goes hand-in-hand with an indifference to what is genuine and valuable in the art of today which is profoundly depressing.

At least there is a point to the biography of a modern writer. I wonder though whether there is any in yet another life of Chaucer or Cervantes when no new facts have come to light to alter the picture. A better idea might be to follow the lead of Hugh Kenner, as Donald Howard is now doing, writing an account not of Chaucer but of the

Chaucer era, 'an X-ray moving picture of how our epoch was created from the medieval', as he puts it, echoing Kenner on Pound. To do that with Cervantes would be to make a genuine attempt to advance our understanding of a great writer, a great period of Spanish art, and a key moment in western civilisation.

The first thing a book conceived on these lines would have to do is to distinguish the important from the trivial. For the truth is that Byron, while producing more than 500 large pages of text, blurs the key fact about Cervantes. This is that he wrote his masterpiece almost accidentally, after failing in most of the accepted literary modes of the time, and that he wrote it at an age when most writers of the day would have been thinking of retirement after a lifetime of service to the Muse. Cervantes was fifty-eight when *Don Quixote*, Part I was published, and he was coming to the end of a hard, sad and pretty unproductive life.

To put it like this is to see that in some important respects Cervantes has more in common with Proust than with Shakespeare or Lope or Ronsard. Because his tone in *Don Quixote* is so cool, so classical, lacking the manic quality of Rabelais or Nashe or the whimsy of Sterne, it is possible to overlook the extraordinary nature of what he is saying. 'Idle reader', his Prologue begins, 'you can believe without any oath of mine that I would wish this book, as the child of my brain, to be the most beautiful, the liveliest and the cleverest imaginable. But I have been unable to transgress the order of nature by which like gives birth to like.' An elegant piece of self-depracatory rhetoric, no doubt, but much more as well. For what Cervantes is doing here is to cast doubt on the very nature of poetic inspiration. In place of the vatic artist, in touch with a transcendental reality, there is only the human being, doing his poor best: 'And so, what could my sterile and ill-cultivated genius beget but the story of a lean, shrivelled, whimsical child, full of variegated fancies that no one else has ever imagined.' Is not this child the Don as well as the book? Is not the greatest of literary characters so lean, so weak, so little able to impose his vision upon the world precisely because he is only a fleshing out of Cervantes' own doubts about his abilities?

Medieval and Renaissance writers had often reflected about their art, but here art itself grows out of its own doubts. 'Calm,' the Prologue continues, 'a quiet place, the pleasantness of the fields, the serenity of the skies, the murmuring of streams and the tranquility of the spirit play a great part in making the most barren muses bear fruit': but for Cervantes there is no such pastoral calm, no space free from the pressures of the world, no time sealed off from the ever passing seconds. The novel is born here, in the ability of prose freed from formal demands to question its own genesis, in the acknowledgement — humorous, unsentimental — of the lie of Art and Imagination upon which all previous literature had been founded.

The extraordinary thing is that this Don Quixote, this lean, shrivelled, whimsical child of Cervantes' brain, whose name is uncertain and his antecedents even more so, who is constantly in danger of reverting to mere marks on a page (think of the way Cervantes freezes and unfreezes him in the fight with the Basque): this Don Quixote is also one of the great 'rounded characters' of world literature. It is as if Cervantes, by letting air into the usually sealed-off space of creation, had enlisted our own imagination on the hero's behalf. And so it comes about that when, on the very last page, we read of 'Don Quixote's weary and mouldering bones' resting in the grave 'where he most certainly lies, stretched at full length and powerless to make a third journey', the final irony of that 'most certainly' only reinforces the weight of his long body which we actually sense for ourselves — while Cervantes, his inventor, for all the efforts of biographers, flies away from us, weightless, insubstantial, to rejoin the millions who have lived and died perhaps not quite in vain.

NOTES

*_Cervantes_, William Byron, Cassell, £9.95

8
Three Thousand Years of Poetry *

It is not often that a reviewer can say that the book under review has altered his entire conception of the past. Yet that is what I have to say about this book.

It is, to begin with, the product of an extraordinary combination of love and scholarship. Not only is it the first anthology of Hebrew verse in any language to run from Biblical times to the present; it is a bilingual anthology, with the Hebrew and the English printed to face each other, and, though the English translations are not in verse, Carmi's prose combines accuracy and grace to such a degree that readers without Hebrew will be able to enjoy this book almost as much as readers with; while those, like myself, who are in the process of learning the language, or have only vague memories of it from their dim childhood past, will find many hours of pleasure awaiting them as they patiently decipher the original with the help of the translations.

But the book is much more than a selection of the best Hebrew poetry of the last three thousand years. Carmi has prefaced the anthology with a fifty-page introduction which is both eminently readable and crammed with information. But even this is not all. The introduction forms only part of the apparatus. In addition, there is a concise essay on medieval Hebrew genres, which directs us to poems and poem-cycles within the anthology; an essay on the systems of Hebrew versification by Benjamin Hrushovsky, which is a model of its kind; a very useful bibliography; and, most interesting of all, a table of contents which is presented in the form of running comments on individual poets and poems. The book does not therefore fall into the usual two distinct parts — an introduction where the facts are presented and the editor explains the reasons for his choices, and an anthology of poems. The way the volume is conceived forces us to move backwards and forwards continually, as a note to Poem A

THREE THOUSAND YEARS OF POETRY

suggests a link with poem B, and a reference in poem B is drawn to our attention and compared to one in poem C, which guides us back to the essay on genres, which in turn sends us out to other poems in the anthology.... There may be other collections of poetry conceived in this way, but I have not come across them; certainly this is a model it would repay any anthologist to study.

The embedding of the poetry in its historical and literary context is of course particularly valuable here, for the double reason that we, to our shame, know so little about the bulk of Hebrew poetry, and that this poetry is more closely tied to one particular book, the Bible, and to the fortunes of the communities which produced the poetry than is the case with any other major literature. The history of Jewish poetry is a unique phenomenon, but its very uniqueness has much to tell us about the very different conditions that have obtained in the literary histories of Japan, Greece, Germany or England.

There are, in fact, four overlapping influences shaping this poetry: that of the Jewish community to which the poet belongs; that of the larger, non-Jewish community in which this is embedded (Moslem Spain, say, or Tsarist Russia); that of other Jewish communities at work elsewhere at the same time; and, of course, the continuing Biblical presence, of paramount importance to a people without a land. One is therefore likely to find conservative poetry written in Babylonia after a model which has not changed for centuries appearing at the same time as startlingly new imitations of Arabic secular poetry in Spain, and as bitter lamentations, modelled on Biblical genres, written in Germany at the time of the terrible pogroms which seemed always to flourish in the wake of the Crusades. Thus, though the anthology is rightly chronological, we have the queer sense not so much of steady movement down the centuries as of eddying waters, spreading further and further afield, but whose source is always present in any sample.

Carmi dedicates the book to Dan Pagis, another Israeli poet and scholar (the two have appeared together in a Penguin Modern Poets volume), and one of the shortest poems in the book is Pagis's 'Written in Pencil in the Sealed Freight Car':

> Here in this carload, I, Eve, with my
> son, Abel. If you see my older boy, Cain,
> the son of Adam, tell him that I

History and Scripture come together here to make this one of the most dignified and moving evocations of that complex series of events we try to make sense of by calling it the Holocaust. How little the poet needs to *say*, but how alive he must be to the vibrations of the past, to the resonance of ancient words and stories. With such a weapon at one's disposal it is fatally easy to cut oneself. The best contemporary Israeli poets, however, have a wonderful ability to handle this potent tradition with a cool off-handedness that is far more resonant than the most grandiose rhetoric. In his introduction, Carmi quotes from a poem by Yehuda Amichai (not included in the volume):

> The man under the fig-tree telephoned the man under his vine: / 'To-night they will surely come. / Armour the leaves, / Lock up the tree, / Call home the dead and be prepared.

And Carmi comments:

> The introduction of the anachronistic telephone into the body of a famous biblical idiom for peace and peace of mind — 'They shall sit every man under his vine and under his fig-tree and none shall make them afraid' — is enough to jolt any Hebrew reader. But something is also happening on the physical, visual level. The peace-loving vine and fig-tree shed their symbolic roles and are transformed into the routine accessories of field camouflage.

Such shedding, such transformation, such irony, he could have added, are the stuff of Hebrew poetry of all periods.

Surprisingly, modern Hebrew poetry has been well served by translations in recent years. Penguin have already brought out English versions of poetry by Nelly Sachs, Abba Kovner, Pagis and Carmi; Tony Rudolf's Menard Press has made available the wonderful poems of Amir Gilboa (to my mind the best living Israeli poet), Yehuda Amichai, Leah Goldberg, Moshe Dor, Shlomo Viner, Dahlia Ravikovitch and David Vogel; Oxford University Press have published Amichai and Carcanet Pagis; Tony Rudolf and Howard Schwarz have recently edited an enormous volume of modern Jewish poetry, which includes a 300-page section on Hebrew poetry (*Voices Within the Ark*, New York, Avon Books, 1980). All these of course are in English only. But some years ago Schocken Books brought out a companion volume to Stanley Burnshaw's splendid *The Poem Itself*, entitled *The Modern Hebrew Poem Itself*. This has the Hebrew and English on facing pages, and seems editorially to have been guided by some of the same principles as lie behind the present volume: at least the names of Carmi, Pagis and Hrushovsky are prominent there too. Many of the poems included in the third section of the Penguin are to be found in the American volume, and in the case of Bialik and Amichai I personally prefer the Schocken selection. But since, as I have been suggesting, no modern Hebrew poet can be understood without a sense of the tradition in which he is working, the Penguin triumphs once again, even if it is only modern poetry one is interested in.

The present volume is divided into three sections: Biblical and post-Biblical, medieval and modern. But in fact it forms a seamless whole. And the first thing to be said about the choice of poems is that it is a poet's choice: every poem is there because it is good. And that makes about 450 pages of good poetry, most of it completely unknown to English readers. What is even more startling is, as I have said, that this is the first comprehensive selection of Hebrew poetry not just in English but even in Hebrew. To understand why this should be so is to gain an insight into the extraordinary way in which the physical and the spiritual seem always to be intertwined in the destiny of this people.

For the simple fact is that much of this poetry was totally unknown a hundred years ago. And I don't mean unknown to the wider public. I mean that it had literally been lost. How it came to be recovered is a story which I find more moving than the discovery of Tutankhamun's treasure or the Palace of Knossos. Let Carmi tell it:

> The enormous jigsaw puzzle of *piyut* [medieval Hebrew poems] began to reveal its contours only with the discovery of the Cairo Genizah ['hiding place']. This momentous event — momentous for almost every branch of Hebrew scholarship — has been aptly described as a cluster of miracles. It was a miracle that the community in Fostat [Old Cairo], which is known to have bought its synagogue in the ninth century, perpetuated the customs and liturgy of the Palestinian rite. It was a miracle that they, and subsequent generations, held the written word in such esteem that any piece of writing in Hebrew could not simply be thrown away, but had to be stored in a special lumber-room. It was a miracle that hundreds of thousands of fragments were deposited in the windowless room in the synagogue's attic from the eleventh to the ninteenth century. And it was nothing less than a miracle that they were preserved from decay and were not discovered prematurely.

THE MIRROR OF CRITICISM

In 1896 two ladies from Cambridge, on a visit to Cairo, bought some Hebrew manuscripts as a memento. On their return they showed them to Solomon Schechter, then reader in Rabbinics at Cambridge University. He realised, to his amazement, that he was looking at a fragment of the Hebrew original of Ecclesiasticus.

Schechter rushed to Cairo and succeeded in obtaining permission to crate some 100,000 fragments back to Cambridge. In an article in *The Times* published in the following year he recorded his impressions of the Genizah:

> It is a battlefield of books, and the literary productions of many centuries had their share in the battle, and their *disjecta membra* are now strewn over its area. Some of the belligerants have perished outright, and are literally ground to dust in the terrible struggle for space, whilst others, as if overtaken by the general crush, are squeezed into big, unshapely lumps, which even with the aid of chemical appliances can no longer be separated without serious damage to their constituents. In their present condition these lumps sometimes afford curiously suggestive combinations; as, for instance, when you find a piece of some rationalistic work, in which the very existence of either angels or devils is denied clinging for its very life to an amulet in which these same beings (mostly the latter) are bound over to be on good behaviour and not to interfere with Miss Jair's love for somebody. The development of the romance is obscured by the fact that the last lines of the amulet are mounted on some I.O.U. or lease, and this in turn is squeezed between the sheets of an old moralist, who treats all attention to money affairs with scorn and indignation. Again, all these contradictory matters cleave tightly to some sheets from a very old Bible.

Whole poets, such as Yannai, one of the greatest of the early medieval masters, were discovered in the Genizah, and many who had hardly been more than names were fleshed out. Even today the bulk of the material has not been properly sifted, and Carmi reminds us that though Samuel Hanagid and Solomon ibn Gabirol are universally recognised as among the greatest Hebrew poets, it was only in 1934 that the bulk of the former's poems was published for the first time, and that over forty unknown poems by the latter were first published only three years ago. That is why Carmi insists that his selection can only be in the nature of an interim report.

THREE THOUSAND YEARS OF POETRY

Yet that statement should not lead us to underestimate the extraordinary achievement which this book represents. For the reader who thinks himself reasonably familiar with the Bible, the biblical selections alone, with the attendant annotations, will come as a salutory shock. 'The beginning of wisdom in biblical study', Carmi quotes Professor Greenberg as saying, 'is the realisation that the Bible is an exotic book about which modern readers understand very little.' How does the Western reader react to the suggestion put forward some years ago by the great biblcal scholar, Umberto Cassuto, that the principles of organisation for the biblical books, as well as for sections within the books, may well include the principle of size: you start with the longest, and end with the shortest? Yet this principle clearly applies to parts of the Koran, and is obviously at work in the lay-out of the Prophetic Books in Scripture. Such a principle, however, runs counter to every possible Western idea of meaning and organisation, with its strong holistic bias. Carmi's notes to his biblical selections place these firmly in their Middle Eastern context, and in doing so remind us that what we had so long taken as utterly familiar may well be utterly alien. The attacks on holism of Nietzsche and Derrida here find factual confirmation; they cease to be strange and radical attempts to force us out of our normal ways of thinking, and make us see that it may simply be that we have for too long ignored a central part of our heritage, or been too selective in our sense of what was our 'tradition'. To give one simple example, which simultaneously illustrates Carmi's genius for the apt quotation from the relevant authority. In his preface he makes the simple factual point that he will translate the second person singular by 'You' or 'you' when referring to the Deity, rather than 'Thou'. He backs this decision by quoting Professor Orlinsky: 'The Biblical writers made no distinction between God on the one hand and man or animal on the other so far as the pronoun or verbal form was concerned. God and the serpent and Pharaoh — all are addressed directly by "*attah*".'

The rich array of post-biblical liturgical poetry here presented should also go some way towards resolving one of the most bitter debates Christian scholars are now engaged in. For the past ten years Michael Goulder has been scandalising conservative theologians by his insistence on the Hebrew liturgy and lectionary as the principle key to the organisation not merely of late Old Testament books like Chronicles, but even of the Gospels and Revelations. Carmi's anthology would seem to lend credence to Goulder's views by revealing how post-biblical poetry, up to the tenth century, was in fact written, usually by cantors, precisely to fit into a still rather open liturgical framework. He is quite right to take the first section of his anthology up to the rise of secular poetry in Spain, for there is actually no sharp break between the Bible and post-biblical liturgical poetry; the decision to close the canon of Scripture and to fix the liturgy once and for all were purely social and political decisions, which had little to do with the content of either scripture or liturgy.

Carmi, of course, had quite enough material from printed sources and he has not ventured into manuscript archives. But it is amazing how much he has uncovered. One of the discoveries he is most pleased about, and rightly, is a tenth-century sequence of poems on the death of Moses, which he found written out as prose in a Bologna rite. Here is the fourth poem in that sequence:

He Refuses to Die
'I will not die! Why should I die?
'If it is because of my perverse words, spoken at the burning bush, when I heard you say, mouth to mouth, "You shall put the words in Aaron's mouth"; when I sinfully answered: "I am slow of speech", and angered You who give man speech — if this is my crime, blot it out and do not call it to mind!'
And the Dread One answered him that very day: 'Your words were sweet to me, and though they faltered at the bush they will be remembered for many generations. How can such words be counted a crime?
'That is not why.'
'If that is not why, why then should I die?'
'Moses, go up and die, for it has been decreed that you shall die!'

Such poems, in their realism and their sweet simplicity, will remind English readers of medieval English poetry, in particular such pieces as the Chester 'Sacrifice of Isaac', so beautifully set by Britten. But there are also, in the long medieval section, passionate or witty love poems modelled on Arabic or Italian secular love poetry, and a number of funny and conceited poems, such as the one on the flea which is made up entirely of biblical quotations and which out-Donnes (out-does?) Donne. Though the poetry is always informed by Scripture it is never pious, and indeed it is often ribald or at least risqué, as in this short poem by Todros Abulafia of Toledo, a contemporary of Dante:

> How terrible, how bitter was the day of your parting, my graceful girl. When I remember it, no part of my body is left unscarred. But how very beautiful were your feet when they twined and climbed my back.

Carmi comments:

> The last line is a typical example of the humour achieved by displacing a biblical phrase. In the original, Lamentations 1:14, the reference is to God's hand which 'plaits' or 'knots' the author's sins about his neck.

One of my own favourites is the sonnet by Ephraim Luzzato, an eighteenth-century doctor appointed physician to London's Portuguese community hospital, whose disregard of religious decorum earned him much criticism. It concerns a rabbi he particularly disliked who had recently been delivered of a kidney stone, and its two rhyme words are, of course, 'stone' and 'water':

> Arise, afflicted master, see how this people, silent as a stone, is here shedding water. At their groans of distress the waters of the sea pile up. Beams cry out from the woodwork, and stones from the wall.
>
> Now, almighty one, give forth a torrent of water and — gently, easily — discharge the stone. The hearts of those about you are melting, flowing away like water. But you, do not lose heart, for yours is stronger than stone.
>
> The merciful God, who once made streams of water run from a rock in the wilderness, will now draw out water for you from His spring of deliverance.
>
> Surely you will remove the stone from the mouth of the well. You will give us waters [of wisdom] to drink, as you did in former days — until the cornerstone is laid on the good Mountain.

In the end, though, this anthology is much more than the sum of its marvellous parts. And that for two reasons. First, despite the variety, a sense of unity does come through. This has nothing to do with common themes, but is a distinctive tone, which can perhaps best be pointed out by quoting two passages, one from the first poem, the 'Song of the Sea' from Exodus: 'I shall sing to the Lord, for He has triumphed gloriously; horse and chariot He has hurled into the sea.' And the other from the contemporary Israeli poet, Hayim Gouri, whose poem 'Heritage' is to be found on p. 565. That poem ends: 'Isaac, as the story goes, was not sacrificed. He lived for many years, saw what pleasure had to offer, until his eyesight dimmed. But he bequeathed that hour to his offspring. They are born with a knife in their hearts.'

Secondly, what this book does is to break up a history that had become monolithic for us, to open doors and windows in what we had thought were blank walls. The history of Spain and of Spanish poetry, of Germany and German poetry, of Italy and Italian poetry — all these will have to be revised and rethought in the light of this book. It alters the context of our thought about the past, reinforcing the insights of such scholars as Peter Brown and Meyer Schapiro, who have tried to draw us out of our Rome-centred, classics-centred view of the past. It truly does what Eliot said every masterpiece did: alters, if ever so slightly, every single work in the tradition.

NOTES

**The Penguin Book of Hebrew Verse*, ed. and trans. T. Carmi, Harmondsworth, 1981, £6.95

9

The Last Great Book*

If Joyce had not existed the professors would have had to invent him. His works cry out for explication, footnoting and the exercise of those crossword puzzle skills at which the academic mind excels. Books on Joyce's novels, like books on Milton's poems, really can help the reader in ways that books on Donne and Eliot, however good they may be, rarely do.

A 'reader's guide' to Joyce is therefore welcome, and when the author is someone as erudite and humane as Matthew Hodgart, it is doubtly welcome. Although the book is short and modest in its intention, it is by no means a mere summary of available scholarship. Hodgart has his own views on a wide variety of issues, is more interested in music than most literary men (a great advantage for the reader of Joyce), and sensibly prefaces his detailed studies of the individual works with analyses of Irish history and literature which are most helpful in placing Joyce in context.

And yet this sort of book makes one uneasy, no matter how talented its author. Compare Hodgart's comment on *Exiles* with Hugh Kenner's. '*Exiles*', writes Hodgart, 'Joyce's only play (1918), is a tribute to his great master Henrik Ibsen, and an exploration of his marital problems. Beyond that, there is not a great deal to say.' Kenner too thinks little of the play, but here is what he chooses to say about it:

> He needed to write something with no point of view, no narrator, whatever: something wholly 'objective': something in which the only point of view would be that of the spectator, making what can be made of the characters when nothing is accessible but their speeches and their behaviour. What happens when the story-teller gets as far outside his story as that? When the writer is Joyce, what happens is that he loses control.

THE MIRROR OF CRITICISM

Kenner, in other words, is not writing a guide, he is presenting a thesis. He does not take the works as a given body of material which simply needs to be charted, but as part of a continuing exploration, a quest which is Joyce's own as well as ours. *Exiles* for him is not just 'Joyce's only play', which needs to be first described and then to have judgement passed on it; it is a choice, a possible direction. By making us see that for Joyce it is the wrong direction he makes us understand the real nature of Joyce's achievement when he finds the right one.

Kenner's thesis, though developed in barely 100 pages, is so rich and suggestive, his writing, as always, so fertile in arresting formulations, that it is impossible to do it justice here. Basically, what he argues is that the so-called 'objective' narrative style of the novel from Defoe to the late nineteenth century, is not in any way natural, but emerges out of a particular ideology, that which holds that 'one word equals one thing', and would banish rhetoric to the realm of falsehood.

He shows Joyce becoming conscious of the problem as early as the first stories in *Dubliners*, seeking to overcome it by always relating even apparently 'objective' narrative to a particular character, and finally, in *Ulysses*, confronting head-on the full implications of his instinctive discovery and turning the voice of narration itself into a character who takes on a larger and larger role as the book progresses, gradually freeing himself from the limits of a purely theoretical verisimilitude, until 'he' emerges fully fleshed out, so to speak, as the incarnation of the Homeric Muse, the untrammelled voice of desire, in the final chapter.

Kenner's thesis is not new, though the English and American academic community still finds it had to grasp. But he distinguishes himself from such critics as Marthe Robert and Roland Barthes by his extraordinary feeling for linguistic nuance. When, for example, he first makes the point that 'the narrative idiom need not be the narrator's', and that Joycean syntax may mirror the priorities of a character whom we needn't necessarily think of as actually framing the sentence, he gives an example:

> The conjunction at the hinge of a sentence about Gerty McDowell's face — 'The waxen pallor of her face was almost spiritual in its ivory-like purity though her rosebud mouth was a genuine Cupid's bow, Greekly perfect.' — is neither an 'and' assembling effects out of pallor and rosebud, nor a 'but' disjoining their allegations (saint's complexion but sinner's lips); it is 'though', and it wobbles like Gerty's half-formed notion that the ivory and the rose, the

THE LAST GREAT BOOK

Spiritual and the Cupidinous, though conventionally incompatible may thanks after all to good taste — *this* sentence cannot be finished.

This is a criticism of a very high order, awareness of detail which springs from an awareness of the ultimate implications of strategy. Kenner's little book (the T. S. Eliot Memorial Lectures for 1977) is a better introduction to Joyce than many a more solid tome; it is a genuine guide because it carries a sense of the ultimate excitement and importance of its subject matter, and that is not just Joyce but literature itself.

Nevertheless, a doubt remains. Not about Kenner, but about Joyce. No objective style, Kenner rightly insists, can be said to exist; no truth can be discovered by aligning so many words to so many things; every attempt to simulate such a Truth will, as in the case of Hemingway, itself quickly become a 'style'. 'The True Sentence, in Joyce's opinion, had best settle for being true to the voice that utters it.' Yet what Kenner fails to see is that in the end Joyce does, against his own deepest insights, cling to one unquestioned Truth, that of the completed work. If there is no True Sentence, then why is there a True Work? This, it seems to me, is a major weakness of Joyce, his refusal to recognise the vulnerability of the Muse, his insistence, against the evidence, that to make a book is itself a valuable activity.

Compared with Proust and Beckett, Kafka and Eliot and Virginia Woolf, Joyce presents a strangely rigid attitude; he refuses ever to let go, to trust the work to take him where it will. Every 'letting go' has to be carefully fitted into its place in the overall design, even though there is no longer, by his own admission, any authority for the pattern the design itself assumes.

It is perhaps a weakness of Joyce and not just a fact about him that he is such a godsend to the academic community. For there is ultimately something cosy and safe about *Ulysses*: underlying it is the belief that the mere accumulation of detail and complexity is an unquestioned good. Far from being 'the decisive English-language book of the [twentieth] century,' as Kenner suggests, it is perhaps the last great book of the nineteenth.

NOTES

* *James Joyce; A Student's Guide*, Matthew Hodgart, Routledge & Kegan Paul, £5.95

Joyce's Voices, Hugh Kenner, Faber, £5.50

10

Life and Letters*

———▸●●━●●◂———

Virginia Woolf was always a slow and painstaking worker. Yet between 1923 and 1928 she wrote *Mrs. Dalloway*, *To the Lighthouse* and *Orlando*; published the first *Common Reader* and delivered the lectures that were to form the basis of *A Room of One's Own*; and began to grope towards the form of *The Waves*. These were, in other words, miraculous years, when, in her forties, she at last began to find her true vein and had the satisfaction of seeing herself, in a short time, achieving international recognition. A volume of letters written in this period thus promises to be enormously exciting. In fact, it is both dull and depressing. What are the reasons for this?

There are, I think, quite a number of them. When Nietzsche remarked that there were only two books worth reading in the German language, Goethe's *Conversations with Eckermann* and Lichtenberg's *Aphorisms*, he was not being merely provocative. What he was, in effect, saying was that he was tired of the well-made work, the polished artefact, that if what one wanted from literature was real insight into the human condition one had to go to the pre-literary, the unformed, to the place where the artist let down his mask and revealed the doubts, hesitations and despair of the self-imposed task. And it is true, I think, that we particularly relish the letters and diaries of artists who give little away in their work, like Flaubert or Kafka, or who, in the nature of things, never talk to us directly — painters and composers. Reading the letters of van Gogh or Schoenberg, we get a vivid sense of the triumph of the spirit in the face of private doubts and public rejection, something that makes us cherish these documents as warmly as we do the paintings and music of their authors.

The letters of Proust, on the other hand, are utterly boring precisely because the doubts and hesitations are so fully explored in *A la Recherche*. And this is equally true of Virginia Woolf. Like Proust, she

LIFE AND LETTERS

wrote fiction not to provide a mirror of the society around her, but to slough off the thick skin of everyday social intercourse, and get through to a more essential self.

The letters are almost exclusively about the social life: helping to raise funds to get Eliot out of his bank; putting off an impending visit by Lady Ottoline Morrell; telling her sister the latest bit of Bloomsbury gossip. Like Proust, Virginia Woolf has a compulsive need for the social life, but only, it would seem, in order to exacerbate her sense of the futility of it all, and to drive her harder in her search for alternative values in her writing. So our frustration at reading this large volume of letters is, in one sense, illuminating: it reflects her own sense of frustration at the innumerable little crises and adjustments which make up daily living, and thus make us more aware of the need to discover a deeper, more satisfying world, where the whole of ourselves would come into play.

Indeed, the best letters in this volume are those to Jacques Raverat as he lay dying in France, and then to his widow. It took death, in her daily as in her imaginative life, to force Virginia Woolf past the ticks and twitchings of social skirmishing into a richer, more human world. Even love could not do this, and the letters to Vita Sackville-West, which take up a large part of this volume, are tedious and embarrassing to a degree, surpassed only by the coy and maudlin letters she wrote to Leonard when she and Vita took a week's holiday together in Burgundy in 1928. The sense of her playing a role, trapped in poses which are not her at all — the 'older woman', the 'helpless child' — is most evident here, as it is, indeed, bound to be in the love letters of someone who in the last resort wished to remain utterly private.

But though the bulk of the volume is both tedious and embarrassing, there are paragraphs here and there for which we must certainly be grateful. It is simply that the whole project of a *Collected Letters* does her a gross disservice. As it happens, I had just been re-reading the letters of Wallace Stevens before I embarked on this volume. For that book, Holly Stevens selected under 1000 letters out of a total of well over 3000, and presented them so that we get the sense in one volume of the whole span of a man's life and of its predominant concerns. It is a profoundly moving book, which should be read by everyone, whether they get on with Stevens's poetry or not, for it provides a record of what one thoughtful and strong-willed man made of his life in a world deprived of its ancient certainties. One of the great pleasures of reading volumes of letters lies in this fact, that they provide one with

85

the sense of the total span of a life, so that one puts them down, as one does a Shakespearian tragedy, full of a sense of awe and wonder. But in the present volume we have almost 600 pages spanning just six years. There is no sense of change or movement at all. Surely those scholars who wish to know about the fortunes of the Eliot fund or what Virginia Woolf thought of Thomas Hardy could go to the three or four libraries which house the bulk of Virginia Woolf MSS and dig about for themselves? For the rest of us, the preponderance of dull and uninteresting material in this volume drives out the good, and we are left with a book that only a sadist would recommend.

Leonard Woolf, after his wife's death, produced a most moving and vivid book out of the mass of diary material. This could surely have provided a model for a 'selected letters'. Instead, we are now faced with the prospect of the publication of the entire diary in five volumes, and six volumes of letters.

Who is all this aimed at? The pious? The prurient? The scholarly? Certainly the publishers must feel that there is a market for such things, and the editors are no doubt sincere in their belief that they are doing a service to the memory of a great writer. In fact, they are doing nothing of the sort. For the supreme irony is that here is a writer whose best work is almost exclusively about loss, failure and despair, about the inability of any of us to hold the threads of our lives together, about the ways we protect ourselves from pain and in the process protect ourselves from life. By managing to give voice to this she makes areas manageable in our lives, and for this reason her greatest novels are among the most exhilarating in the language. But now this mass of secondary material threatens to make her safe, respectable, someone of whom we can say, as Wallace Stevens said of Arp, 'The human spirit has nothing to fear from him.'

The editors are scrupulous in the performance of their task, but they have betrayed their subject. On the very first page, for example, we read, in the note to the first batch of letters, that 'having published *Jacob's Room*, her first experimental novel, in October 1922, she was making slow progress with *Mrs. Dalloway*'. This is not scholarly objectivity, it is the perpetuation of damaging myths. For Virginia Woolf was not more or less 'experimental' than Tolstoy or George Eliot or Turgenev (on whom she always wrote well, as witness the essay in Mary Lyon's useful collection of some of her reviews from 1904 to 1928). Like them, she was concerned only with expressing as precisely as possible what it was she wanted to say.

LIFE AND LETTERS

No one, surely, supposes that George Eliot or Turgenev started at page one of their novels and wrote steadily through to the end. Every artist experiments in his study, trying out a sentence or a scene this way and that until he is satisfied. Virginia Woolf was merely satisfied a little less easily than most of her contemporaries. If we are prepared to re-read the novels and open ourselves up to them instead of imagining that we can 'understand' her by reading more and more about her and around her, we would recognise this. And we would realise that there are so few artists in any generation who go on being important to us after their death that we need to be very careful what we do to those that are.

NOTES

*A Change of Perspective: The Letters of Virginia Woolf, vol. III, ed. Nigel Nicolson, Hogarth, £12.50

Books and Portraits: Some Further Selections from the Literary and Biographical Writings of Virginia Woolf, ed. Mary Lyon, Hogarth, £5.50

11

Saneness and Wisdom *

>─●─●─●─●─<

We have long known that Kafka was an extraordinary letter-writer. The sixty-page letter to his father, and the heart-rending letters to Milena, have for years been part of the Kafka canon. Then in 1974 came the English translation of the letters to Felice Bauer, the girl he was twice engaged to. Now, with the publication here of the letters he wrote from 1900 to his death in 1924 we at last have the chance to take full stock of Kafka, to see him in a wide range of different moods, and to follow his brief tragic life in his own words rather than having to rely on Brod's quaint biography.

The majority of the letters are, of course, those to Brod himself; but we also find here letters to other friends such as Oskar Pollack and Robert Klopstock, and the Prague writers Oskar Baum and Felix Weltsch; to his publisher Kurt Wolff; to numerous girls and women; and of course to his sisters. Only the letters to his favourite sister Ottla are missing, and they have been collected together in a separate volume and will presumably soon appear in English.

The first 'letter' published here is an entry in a girl's album. It dates from September 1900, when Kafka was seventeen. 'How many words in this book,' he has written. 'They are meant for remembrance. As though words could carry memories. For words are clumsy mountaineers and clumsy miners. Not for them to bring down treasures from the mountains' peaks or up from the mountains' bowels.' We see at once that there is no question with Kafka of a gradual discovery of style and subject-matter, and indeed the letters to Oskar Pollack which follow are among the richest and most exciting of the whole collection. When one realises that they were written at the age of nineteen it is evident that, whatever terrible sufferings he experienced in the course of his life, Kafka was from the first blessed with genius. It is quite simply impossible for him to write anything trivial or unoriginal. 'I sat at my fine desk...' he writes to Pollack,

SANENESS AND WISDOM

it's a respectably-minded desk which is meant to educate. Where the writer's knees usually are, it has two horrible wooden spikes. And now pay attention. If you sit down quietly, cautiously at it, and write something respectable, all's well. But if you become excited, look out — if your body quivers ever so little, you inescapably feel the spikes in your knees, and how that hurts. I could show you the black-and-blue marks. And what that means to say is simply: 'Don't write anything exciting and don't let your body quiver while you write.'

But how could Kafka heed the warning? His writing is more physical, more bodily and quivering than that of any other writer. The little anecdote of the desk, recounted so lightly and ironically, hangs like a tiny warning over the life to come. All we have to do is sit back and wait for it to unfold.

And Kafka too knows that he is waiting for something. In 1904 Brod replaces Pollack as close friend and confidant, and already in the second letter to him Kafka touches on this theme:

> It is so easy to be cheerful at the beginning of summer. One has a lively heart, a reasonably brisk gait, and can face the future with a certain hope.... And when people ask us about the life we intend to live, we form the habit, in Spring, of answering with an expansive wave of the hand, which goes limp after a while, as if to say that it was ridiculously unnecessary to conjure up such things.

But the very wealth of possibilities suggests unease; the gesture freezes, the words cease to come and the question has to be faced: with so many possible lives ahead, how is one to choose the right one?

There are three stages in Kafka's journey to an answer, which is also the journey to his death. The first, described in this letter, ends in the Summer of 1912 with the meeting with Felice. The second is the period of Felice, when he discovers his true vocation as a writer and at the same time realises that it is impossible for him to fulfil the wishes of his father and his own deepest desires, and marry. The third opens with his almost relieved letter to Felice in September 1917 telling her of his haemorrhage and of the necessity for them to part, and it lasts until his death.

The Felice episode was the real turning-point in Kafka's life, as he saw quite clearly when he wrote to Brod from Riva where he had escaped after breaking off his first engagement: 'I cannot live with her and I cannot live without her. By this one act my life, which was at least in part mercifully veiled from myself, is now completely unveiled.' And when his illness is finally diagnosed he knows better than anyone what it means: 'I have come to think that tuberculosis, or the kind of tuberculosis I have, is no special disease, or not a disease that deserves a special name, but only the germ of death itself.'

There is both dread and relief at the gradual closing of all the doors. 'Dearest Max,' he writes in 1922, 'I have been dashing about or sitting as petrified as a desperate animal in his burrow.' Literature, which in his youth he had seen as the essential form of salvation, he now recognises as a form of damnation, a contract with the Devil, because, as he writes in his darkest letters to Brod, it is yet one more way of evading reality. 'Our alleged "inferiority"', he writes to Robert Klopstock, 'consists in this, that we are desparate rats who hear the footsteps of the master of the house and flee in various directions — for instance towards women, you toward this one or that one, I toward literature.'

And yet the contradiction remains. He cannot free himself from the habit of writing, or from a belief in it. Even when he is dying, no longer able to speak because of the tuberculosis of the larynx that has got him in its grip, he busily corrects the proofs of his last stories, those miraculous tales that spell out the folly of all tales. And here at the end, as though to crown the exemplary or iconic quality of his life, it is through the written and not the spoken word that he is forced to communicate with those around him. The slips of paper on which he scribbled his messages were preserved by Robert Klopstock, who was with him to the end, and they form an unbearable coda to the volume. One reads: 'How wonderful that is, isn't it? The lilac — dying, it drinks, goes on swilling.' And another: 'Put your hand on my forehead for a moment to give me courage.'

I have isolated the central theme running through these letters, but it would be a mistake to think that they are all of this intensity. Indeed, part of their fascination lies in the fact that we can glimpse here as nowhere else in Kafka certain very human qualities. For one thing he is extremely funny. He writes to Brod in 1909 about his job in the Workers' Accident Insurance Institute:

> I've got so much to do! In my four districts — apart from all my other jobs — people fall off the scaffolds as if they were drunk, or fall into the machines, all the beams topple, all embankments give way,

all ladders slide, whatever people carry up falls down, whatever they hand down they stumble over. And I have a headache from all these girls in porcelain factories who incessantly throw themselves down the stairs with mounds of dishware.

In 1917 he writes to Brod and his wife about a popular singer of the time:

> In comparing him to a pig, I mean no insult.... Have you ever looked as carefully at a pig as at W.?.... The pig's body is not dirty, the animal could even be called fastidious (although this is not the kind of fastidiousness you would want to embrace). He has elegant, delicately stepping feet, and the movements of his body seem to flow from a single impulse. Only his noblest organ, his snout, is hopelessly piggish.

The letters too show considerable interest in the literature of the past and of the present. It is important to remember that though today Brod is known only as Kafka's friend, at the time it was he who was the major writer, pouring out a spate of successful novels, plays and essays. Kafka looked on from the sidelines, often applauding, but also, very quietly, pointing out his unease with aspects of his friend's work. 'I think that certain wrong tracks are followed, ' he writes to Brod about his play *Esther*. 'Even though they may strengthen the play as a work of art... there is something in me that refuses to take these wrong tracks because they represent a sacrifice to art, and are harmful to you.' Brod, we understand, has sacrificed the truth of his intuition to the requirements of the well-made play acceptable at the time. Kafka is much harsher about Gerhard Hauptmann: '*Anna* also somewhat depressed me and at any rate gave me little pleasure... I recognise the master's touch in the structure, in the witty and animated dialogue, in many passages, but the whole thing is such a bag of wind!... one's sense of one's own poor life is certainly enhanced when confronted with such wretched waxworks,' and to Oskar Baum, who had sent him his story, 'The Monster', he writes:

> Dear Oskar, I read it through the same evening, with terror, terror-stricken by that steely animal.... I suppose such things occur to all of us, but who can do it as you do? I ineffectually tried it too, years ago, but instead of groping my way to the desk I preferred to crawl under the sofa, where I can still be found.... I felt the beginning

was a little too busy with externalities, too much hotel and detective stuff. But it's hard to say whether it should be different; perhaps that is just what is needed.

What a gap one senses between the inevitable mediocrity surrounding Kafka and his own modest and luminous genius. He writes to Brod in 1921, when Brod was in the midst of a love affair that threatened to ruin his marriage: 'When the news about you, Felix and Oskar is all set down, and I compare myself with you others, it seems to me that I am wandering like a child in the forests of maturity.' But perhaps it is the adults who have lost their way. The child looks out at us, frightened, guilty, but in possession of something we dare not lay claim to. As Kafka said in one of these early letters to Oskar Pollack: 'Some books seem like a key to unfamiliar rooms in one's own castle.' This is such a book.

NOTES

*ractor;*Letters to Friends, Family and Editors*, Franz Kafka, trans. Richard and Clara Winston, John Calder, £19.50

12

Radiance and Interpretation *

When Kafka died in 1924 not one of his novels had been published. He was known to a small circle — though Janouch's testimony shows that that circle spread beyond his friends — as the author of a story about a man who turned into a beetle. Brod published *The Trial* in 1925, and followed it with *The Castle* (1926), *America* (1927), and a volume of short fragments and aphorisms, *The Great Wall of China* (1931). The first work of Kafka's to be translted into English was *The Castle*, which the Muirs brought out in 1930. In the twenty years following his death, Kafka came to be known in Europe and America simply as the author of *The Trial* and *The Castle*. Those twenty years saw the destruction of the world Kafka had known, and his family with it, and they were years when it might have been thought Europe would have other things on its mind than the assimilation of the strange imaginative world of a Prague Jew writing in German. But it didn't work like that. The very temper of those years made Kafka seem profoundly relevant and prophetic, and by the end of the war his reputation was as solidly established as that of Eliot or Joyce or Proust.

Yet the fact that it was a reputation based largely on the two novels did not really help Kafka. The novels had been edited by Brod according to his views of what Kafka was up to, and were prefaced by Brod's interpretations. In the English versions the Muirs pretty faithfully followed the Brod line — which was more or less to see Kafka as a modern Bunyan. Like all interpretations of Kafka, this one has a good deal of truth in it. One cannot read a page of Kafka without feeling that there is a strong religious sensibility at work, allied to the kind of violent honesty of which no more than a handful of writers are capable in any generation. Nevertheless, those who had come to know and love the works must have felt uneasy with this view, and here and there voices began to be raised which resisted such an interpretation, and insisted on the ultimately mysterious and ambiguous texture of Kafka's art. Chief among these were the voices of Walter Benjamin, Maurice Blanchot, Marthe Robert and Erich Heller. Heller's essay on *The Castle* in *The Disinherited Mind* (1952) marked a real turning-point. He argued persuasively that it was folly to go on debating whether Kafka was religious or anti-religious, Marxist or bourgeois, Calvinist or existentialist. For Kafka's work is not the passive object of interpretation: it is itself actively concerned with the nature of interpretation, and is thus its own best commentary. This Archimedean revolution in the understanding of Kafka in a sense put paid to Kafka studies. There seemed to be nothing more to say. A few i's might still need dotting and a few t's crossing, but by and large the business of Kafka criticism was at an end. And yet, though in some senses Heller was right, he did leave the reader of Kafka with the feeling that something was missing: that more could and should be said. But how? Kafka, as Marthe Robert has remarked in her brilliant new book on Kafka's relation to Judaism, *Seul, comme Franz Kafka*, was never interested in ideas, only in people. It was the actor Löwy and the members of his troupe, not their ideas, which fascinated him; Steiner the man, picking his nose as he enlarged on his views, rather than the views themselves, which he felt constrained to comment on in his diary. And so with Kafka himself. There was something about the man which transcended the works, a quality which one glimpsed through the works, and which could neither be pinned down nor reduced to a simple (or complex) issue about interpretation.

At the time it seemed difficult to bring this quality into focus. Was our curiosity about Kafka any different from our curiosity about Joyce or Scott Fitzgerald? It was, but how and why? Answers to these questions began to emerge as more and more of his writings began to appear: his diaries, his letter to his father, the batch of letters to Milena Jesenska and, finally, the enormous volume of letters to Felice Bauer, the woman he was twice engaged to and who, with his father, was surely the central external factor in his life. Of the twelve volumes of Kafka's writings in the German edition, just over half are devoted to what might be called 'non-fiction'. But the strange thing about these letters and diaries was not that they made us realise how much more autobiographical the novels were than we had thought, but that they forced us to revise our notions of where the boundaries might lie between fiction and non-fiction. They did not so much open Kafka up to us as give us a great many more examples of his perennial

RADIANCE AND INTERPRETATION

mysteriousness. And suddenly it seemed possible to talk about Kafka, the man and the work, without falling either into the Brod-Muir trap or into the self-descructiveness of the Heller approach. There was a whole world waiting to be explored, and which could be explored with humanity and patience: the world of Kafka's relations with people, with his background, with his art. A new, much more varied Kafka was emerging, a human, frequently humorous Kafka, alive to the world around him, and not merely obsessed with inner anguish.

This book is a celebration of that Kafka. Its epigraph could well be this sentence from Roy Fuller's splendid essay, which sets out to overturn Brod's view that Kafka's daily stint at the Insurance Office was totally destructive: 'There are advantages', Fuller writes, 'in a life, however disagreeable, that constantly pits such a writer against the varieties of the everyday — such as are displayed by office life in a large organisation.' The book contains fascinating essays of a strictly biographical nature, studies of Kafka's Prague and of his relations with women. It also contains poems by D.J. Enright and Jerzy Peterkiewicz (not the best works of either), and stories by Philip Roth and the editor on what might have been: A Kafka alive in America after the war, a bachelor schoolmaster; alive in the war and fighting with the partisans. These are not merely *jeux d'esprit*. By making us imagine what might have been they lend depth and poignancy to what in fact was. For if Kafka could have survived his illness and the Nazis, it is possible that such a survival would have meant the loss to the world of the greatest part of his writings; his fastidiousness and his growing sense of art as the essential sin might have led him to destroy all that in fact passed into Brod's safekeeping. In such a way are motives and events tangled and confused.

There are also more standard essays and meditations on Kafka's art by Roy Pascal, Erich Heller, Idris Parry, Tony Thorlby and Walter Sokel. But even these seem to have been lifted above the norm for such essays by the editor's humanity and enthusiasm, and they all have a relaxed and sparkling quality rare in Kafka criticism, an exuberance and a willingness to abandon the central argument for the apparently peripheral insight which makes every paragraph exciting and thought-provoking.

Joyce Crick's essay on Kafka and the Muirs is typical of the spirit of the book. The subject does not sound very promising, yet we get a splendid study not just of the Englishing of Kafka but of a whole range of problems and issues of quite general significance. There is, for example, the question of a minority language, so central to Kafka, which, she points out, was also of prime significance for the Muirs, coming as they did from Shetland and Orkney. There is the question of the almost inevitable bias of the literary imagination of these islands (despite Dickens and Eliot) towards the rural, the natural, which exerts its pull, however faithful the Muirs try to be to Kafka's drab, urbanised language and imagery: the flimsy *leichtgebautes Haus*, where Georg Bendemann lives, is ruinously 'ramshackle' in English. The pallid *schwaches Grün* he looks out onto becomes a warm and spring-like 'tender green'. And the picture Crick gives of central Europe in the interwar period is particularly good just because she is not directly concerned with that: we only glimpse it out of the corner of the eye, so to speak. How fascinating, and what a splendid instance of the evocative power of detail, to learn that a chance meeting with Willa's old friend A. S. Neil led to the Muirs moving to join his experimental school at Hellerau — the very school to which Kafka had urged his sister Elli to send her ten-year-old son: 'You should send young Felix there. It will save him from the mean, lukewarm, squinnying spirit so strong in well-off Prague Jews.'

The same ability to speak seriously about Kafka without turning him into Modern Man or The Artist, is to be found in Roy Fuller's essay. Fuller rightly compares Kafka with that other insurance lawyer, Wallace Stevens, who, when the time came to retire, insisted on carrying on, since he felt that only by having his regular, quite unpoetical job to fill up his day could he go on being the instinctive and prolific writer he was. And he quotes Stevens's marvellous letter of 17 February 1930 to Thomas McGreevy, which should be pinned above every fretful writer's desk:

> If Beethoven could look back on what he had accomplished and say that it was a collection of crumbs compared to what he had hoped to accomplish, where should I ever find a figure of speech adequate to size up the little that I have done compared to that which I had once hoped to do? Of course, I have had a happy and well-kept life. But I have not even begun to touch the spheres within spheres that might have been possible if, instead of devoting the principal amount of my time to making a living, I had devoted it to thought and poetry. Certainly it is as true as it ever was that whatever means most to one should receive all of one's time and that has not been true in my case. But, then, if I had been more determined about it, I

might now be looking back not with a mere sense of regret but at some actual devastation. To be cheerful about it, I am now in the happy position of being able to say that I don't know what would have happened if I had had more time. This is very much better than to have had all the time in the world and have found oneself inadequate.

And yet there is a danger in this sort of argument. It can all too easily turn from a critique of banal Romanticism to a vindication of smug mediocrity. Would Joyce have been better off with an office job? Would Proust? I mean no disrespect to Roy Fuller in asking if Virginia Woolf is not a better novelist than he, or Rilke a better poet. But I feel the issue needs to be raised, because it is one that goes to the heart of this whole collection. Salutary and welcome though it is, it is perhaps in danger of assimilating Kafka a little too readily to a cosy pragmatism which is characteristic of the best and worst in English letters. There is a perfect example of what I mean in Professor Stern's own admirable introduction. He says: 'There is about the man Franz Kafka a charm, a good-natured resignation, an uncommon kindness and thoughtfulness for others, which comes across in his letters and in the testimonies of friends... there is, every now and then, a mocking exasperation with himself and a gentle sense of humour... a humour which should not bear the brunt of "deep" interpretation.' He then proceeds to give examples of this sense of humour, including the following:

> On a rainy day in Marienbad Kafka watches a famous rabbi with his solemn entourage in search of medicinal waters after the springs have all been shut for the day, the bottle brought for the purpose meanwhile filling with rain water — a Marx Brothers scenario which Kafka ends with a comment on one of the rabbi's followers who 'tries to find or thinks he finds a deeper meaning in all this: I think the deeper meaning is that there is none, and in my opinion that is enough'.

This would seem to be justification enough for Stern's general remarks. But the actual letter may not quite bear out his interpretation. Kafka writes:

> He [the rabbi] inspects everything, but especially the buildings; the most obscure trivialities interest him. He asks questions, points out all sorts of things. His whole demeanour is marked by admiration

and curiosity. All in all, what comes from him are the inconsequential comments and questions of itinerant royalty, perhaps somewhat more childish and more joyous. At any rate they reduce all thinking on the part of his escort to the same level. Langer tries to find or thinks he finds a deeper meaning in all this: I think that the deeper meaning is that there is none and in my opinion this is quite enough. It is absolutely a case of divine right, without the absurdity that an inadequate basis would give to it.

This is altogether more mysterious. Kafka talks about the holy rabbi of Belz just as he does about his father. There is nothing in his outward appearance or his actions which would indicate holiness. On the contrary. Yet that is precisely what is so terrifying and authoritative about him. His very childishenss is proof of the gap that lies between him and us. He is imbued with a totally mysterious power and authority, whose source we can never hope to understand. All we can say for certain is that we don't have it. He moves lightly, like a child or a king, with no tension between inner and outer. Only we, like Kafka, carry our burden with us: the need to relate the two, the need to interpret.

I feel that the new, human Kafka Stern is offering us is in danger of turning into a Hume or Dr Johnson, of being assimilated to the temper of English thought in rather the same way that Wittgenstein was assimilated for a while. That may be a necessary stage in our attempt to see him for what he is. Meanwhile, his radiance shines for us as the holy rabbi's did for him: he is a presence in our midst, and will remain untouched by any act of appropriation on our part. This splendid book does a great deal to bring that presence to life.

NOTES

* *The World of Franz Kafka*, ed. J. P. Stern, Weidenfeld, £9.95

13

A Ghost in the City*

Slowly Walter Benjamin's work is filtering through into English. First there was the run-away success of the selection of essays, *Illuminations*; this was followed by two volumes of essays and fragments which Benjamin had amassed on Baudelaire and Brecht, and by the massive thesis, *the Origin of German Tragic Drama*; and now we have a collection of his more intimate, autobiographical writings, plus one or two of the major essays which had not yet appeared in English, notably the one on Karl Kraus.

Like his contemporary Franz Rosenzweig, Benjamin spent his life arguing against essentialism: 'There is no "essence of Judaism"; there is only "Hear, O Israel!"' Rosenzweig had written, and though Benjamin does not on the surface seem at all concerned with the humanistic Judaism of Buber or Rosenzweig, his essays on Kafka, on Brecht's epic theatre, on the story-teller, on the work of art in an age of mechanical reproduction, all repeat the same lesson: we cannot grasp the essence of a work, a person, a landscape; instead, we have to respect its distance and listen to it. Not only that. It was with the Renaissance and the Reformation, with the rise of the novel and the growing embourgeoisement of Europe in the nineteenth century that the idea gained common ground that we might, with a great enough effort, be able to arrest time, freeze the work of art, understand it and the universe once and for all. Benjamin will have none of that. The Essentialism and the notion of a final knowledge is a myth, a mirage. The task of criticism, like that which Brecht assigned to his epic theatre, is to break into the continuum of history and thus reveal its possibilities.

In life this means that he who would understand must not sit silent and contemplate, but must walk. *A Berlin Childhood, One-Way Street*, the essays on Naples, Moscow, Marseilles, all in this volume, testify to Benjamin's lifelong obsession with cities, and his belief that the only way to understand not only them but ourselves is to walk through them. For the way to free yourself from the crushing burden of an insistent time is to transform it into space; this is what the baroque dramatists he studied in *The Origin of German Tragic Drama* did, and this is what he himself, in his own very different way, was drawn to do.

Benjamin recalls how his mother would take him for walks through Berlin and try to 'turn insignificant items of conduct into tests of his aptitude for practical life', as Susan Sontag puts it in her splendid introduction. But this only reinforced Benjamin in his ineptitude, his dreamy and impractical nature. 'My habit of seeming slower, more maladroit, more stupid than I am, had its origin in such walks, and has the great attendant danger of making me think myself quicker, more dexterous, shrewder than I am.' It is as if he had determined to reverse Gargantua's educational process. It will be remembered that Rabelais's giant first had the pleasure of being taught by a scholastic who let him do more or less what he liked; his father then imposed upon him a terrifyingly efficient Renaissance Humanist, who made sure that not an hour of the child's day was wasted. Scholars have never had any doubts that Rabelais was on the side of the Humanist, but Benjamin was a scholar with a difference, and he made it his task to question the assumptions of 400 years of the cultural establishment. Waste, for him, is where life is, and efficiency, the straight road from A to B, is the road of death and suffocation. Hence his love for Baudelaire, that great *flaneur*, and his own lifelong addiction to wandering the streets and passageways of great cities. To know how to wander is to know that time is on your side, to surprise linearity by finding new ways across already well-known terrain. In the same way Benjamin wanders through the works of Kafka and Proust and Baudelaire, surprising us by his unexpected juxtapositions, breaking the linearity to reveal the possibility which lies dormant in each phrase, each image.

The more of Benjamin one reads the more of a piece he seems to be. His mania for collecting, his love of quotation, his restlessness, his wandering in city streets, all are connected, all make sense in terms of the injunction not to look for an essence but rather to respond to the aura, the thisness, the otherness, of an object, a work of art, a person. Nevertheless, these autobiographical writings leave me at any rate slightly uneasy, dissatisfied. It is as if Benjamin needed the mediation of a great artist before his own character could come through. Compared to Proust or to Kafka's letters and diaries, *One-Way Street*

A GHOST IN THE CITY

and *A Berlin Childhood* seem limp, lacking in resonance; curiously, they seem less personal than his critical essays. What is the reason for this? It may be that a Kafka, a Proust, a Klee, were as aware as Benjamin that rather than seek an essence we must constantly make and remake objects which will allow us to get a grip on the world. But their movement comes out of statis: those three artists must have spent more than half their waking lives alone in their rooms, writing or painting. Klee did not take himself for a walk; he took his line. For writing and painting are also a kind of movement, a perpetual *flanerie*. But Benjamin seems to have lacked the self-confidence for this; or perhaps we must simply say that he did not have the artist's urge to make. There is a peace at the heart of even Kafka's deep rootlessness and restlessness, whereas Benjamin seems to be perpetually dissatisfied, wandering from Berlin to Paris to Marseilles to Capri, picking up this bit of work and then that, making one attempt on his life in 1930 and then succeeding at his second attempt, ten years later, as the Germans closed in and he fled to the Spanish border. Perhaps his melancholy and his desire for movement were one, and both sprang from an inability to realise himself in his writing, allied to the profound belief that if there was salvation anywhere it was in his writing.

There is something oddly selfish and cold about Benjamin. His collecting mania, the failure of his marriage, his interest in children's books but not in children — all this makes of him a very different figure from Kafka or Proust or Klee. Perhaps it is this very self-regarding quality, paradoxically, which makes him so much more shadowy a figure than those great creators. Our inability to focus clearly on him may not be the result of lack of familiarity or of the vagaries of translation and publication. He has too much of Swann and too little of Marcel; in many ways he was closer to a collector like Aby Warburg than to the artists he most loved; they gave without stint, and, as Mallarmé said of Poe, eternity has changed them, for us, into themselves. Benjamin held back too much, and as a result he only haunts us as a ghost, as perhaps he goes on haunting the city he was brought up in, Berlin, and the city he loved above all others, Paris.

NOTES

*One-Way Street, Walter Benjamin, New Left Books, £10.75

14

A Childish Vision *

On 19 November 1942, Bruno Schulz, a Jewish teacher of art in the high school of Drohobycz, a small town in south-eastern Poland, was shot dead in the street in the course of a minor SS raid. Eight years earlier rather hesitantly, he had published his first book of stories, *Cinnamon Shops*, which won him immediate recognition in Polish literary circles. This was followed in 1937 by a second collection, the book under review; he also translated Kafka's *The Trial*, and was said to have completed a major novel, *The Messiah*, at the time of his death. Like his body, it has never been found.

In the late 1950s and 1960s, largely owing to the labours of the Polish essayist and poet, Jerzy Ficowski, who tracked down his letters, edited them, and wrote a book about him, Schulz began to be known in the West. Today he is translated into German, French, Italian and Norwegian. *Cinnamon Shops* came out in English last year under the title *The Street of the Crocodiles*, and now Hamish Hamilton have issued his second book, illustrated with his own drawings.

Are we in the process of rediscovering a major talent? It would be nice to be able to say so. And Schulz's solitary life (he never married); his quiet exploration of his craft far from the centres of intellectual ferment; his ambiguous relations with his Jewish origins and the Polish language in which he wrote; above all his tragic and meaningless end — all this is the stuff of which legends are made. It is easy to understand why someone like Focowski or Bashevis Singer should feel strongly about Schulz and should speak of him as a Polish Proust or Kafka. Unfortunately the truth of the matter is that he is not in that class at all. There can be no doubt about his talent or the seriousness of his dedication or the pathos of his end. But this must not blind us to his limitations.

All his work is filled with the richness and wonder of the child's view

A CHILDISH VISION

of reality. Nearly every story deals with childhood in the family home, with his mother, his uncles, Adela the maid, and, above all, his extraordinary eccentric father, a Drogobych merchant who had inherited a textile business and ran it until illness forced him to abandon it to the care of his wife while he retired to ten years of idleness and the world of his dreams. How far this is autobiography and how far it is fiction it is impossible to say, nor is it very important, for Schultz was quite clear that what he wanted to do was to raise the ordinary and humdrum lives of his people and his town to the level of myth. 'I do not know just how in childhood we arrive at certain images, images of crucial significance to us,' he wrote to Witkkiewicz. 'They are like filaments in a solution around which the sense of the world crystallises for us.... They are meanings that seem predestined for us, ready and waiting at the very entrance of our life.' It is the artist's task to try and recapture these images without destroying them in the process. And Schultz has a marvellous gift for evoking the wonder and terror of the most ordinary experiences: a walk through the snow, the smell of a Spring night, the empty rooms of a big house. Anything he turns his attention to is at once seen as far more extraordinary and mysterious than we, set in our adult habits, could possibly have imagined.

But, for the reader, page after page of such evocation can grow tedious, however much it means to Schulz himself. And as a writer too he sensed that there was a problem: 'It is part of my existence to be the parasite of metaphors, so easily am I carried away by the first simile that comes along,' he writes in one of the stories. 'Having been carried away, I have to find my difficult way back and return to my senses.' If the imagination has the power to transmute reality at all times and places, what is going to act as a brake on it? The stories all start from the concrete and specific, then grow more and more wildly surrealistic as image generates image and the plot, freed from the shackles of verisimilitude, careers wildly in all directions. Inevitably, the climax is death, disintegration, apocalypse:

> 'Boys, help, help!' I shouted, already suspended in the air. I could still see their outstretched arms and their shouting, open mouths, but the next moment I turned a somersault and ascended in a magnificent parabola. Breathless I saw in my mind's eye how my schoolmates raised their arms and called out to the instructor: 'Please, sir, please, Simon has been swept away!' The instructor

looked at them from under his spectacles. He went slowly over to the window, and, screening his eyes with his hands, scanned the horizon. But he could not see me. In the dull glare of the pale sky his face had the colour of parchment. 'We must cross his name off the register,' he said with a bitter smile and returned to the rostrum. I was carried higher and higher into the unexplored yellow space.

Schulz, as one can see, attempts to control his fantasy by a kind of irony. Unfortunately the irony does not bite very deep, it remains a merely literary device by means of which he tries to keep the balance between imagination and reality. A comparison with Kafka is illuminating here. Kafka too started by writing first-person narratives in which the whim of the hero could alter the reality of his surroundings. But he quickly gave that up and found his true vein in exploring the contradiction between our sense of ourselves and the world's sense of us. The horror of *Metamorphosis*, for example, comes from the remorseless exploration of the paradox the reader is made to live out from the first sentence on: How can I be *both* myself *and* a beetle? In comparison 'Father's Last Escape', in which Father turns into a crab and is eventually boiled by Mother, suffers not merely from being derivative, but from the arbitrary nature of the event.

Schulz is probably closer to a fine minor writer like Rober Walser (much admired by Kafka of course) than to Kafka himself. Perhaps he was the victim of his time and place. Though no untutored genius (he was a fervent admirer of Mann and Rilke), his very solitude was perhaps his undoing. Art for him was clearly an essential relief from the tedium of his life, and it is therefore natural that he should have placed great faith in it. But, ultimately, it was this very confidence in art and the child's vision which let him down, while Kafka's doubts (like Proust's) are what propelled him towards his major psychological and technical discoveries.

Yet there are moments, in this volume, of magical achievement. In the first story, 'The Book', we learn of a wondrous volume which had brightened his childhood 'with its gentle glow'. It vanishes, but the child refuses to be put off by his father's attempts to convince him that it never existed. One day, entering an empty room, he finds Adela idly leafing through a large tome, and looks over her shoulder:

> On a large folio page there was a photograph of a rather squat and short woman with a face expressing energy and experience. From her head flowed an enormous stole of hair, which fell heavily down

her back, trailing its thick ends on the ground.... It was hard to imagine that its burden was not painful to carry, that it did not paralyse the head from which it grew. But the owner of this magnificence seemed to bear it proudly, and the caption printed under the picture told the history of that miracle, beginning with the words: 'I, Csillag, born at Karlovice in Moravia, had a poor growth of hair...'

What it is is an advertisement for a lotion which is supposed to restore fertility to the scalp! Having applied it, 'she began to grow hair, and, what is more, her husband, brothers, even cousins were covered overnight with a healthy black coating of growth. On the reverse of the page Anna Csillag was shown, six weeks after the prescription was revealed to her, surrounded by her brothers, brothers-in-law, and nephews, bewhiskered men with beards down to their waists, exposed to the admiration of the beholders.' The intermixture of charlatanry and miracle, which is never far from genuine folk culture, has rarely been more accurately and humorously caught. At his best Bruno Schulz can give us something we cannot find in any other modern writer.

NOTES

*Sanatorium under the Sign of the Hourglass, Bruno Schulz, trans. Celina Wieniewska, Hamish Hamilton, £5.95

15
A Happy Man*

In recent years we had come to take Nabokov somewhat for granted. Now he is dead we realise how important he was to us: an example in our compromising times of a man who lived his life in the service of an ideal, and who found happiness even in the darkest periods of human history in the fruitful exercise of his enormous gifts.

He entered our consciousness in the late 1950s with the publication of *Lolita*, and even today, it is difficult to grasp that his first novel appeared as long ago as 1926, only a year after Virginia Woolf's *Mrs. Dalloway*. Looking back, with the help of this biography, we can see that *Lolita* has its roots in the 1920s and 1930s, and that without the dozen or so major works that preceded it, it would never have been the masterpiece it is.

Yet Nabokov always insisted that his best work was to be found in his Russian novels, that with the loss of his mother-tongue he lost the better part of himself. Unlike Joyce and Beckett, he did not choose exile voluntarily; indeed, like so many Russians, he regarded the loss of his native country as a disaster from which he could never be expected wholly to recover. And yet, as we can now see, the vagaries of history made him into the great writer he became, against his will and in ways he was never, I think, quite prepared to recognise.

For Nabokov would have remained a minor writer, nostalgically celebrating the glories of childhood, had the Revolution not made him aware of the nature of loss, and the Nazi threat not made it necessary for him to leave the closed world of Berlin *emigré* society and forced him to come to terms with the otherness of the English language and American culture. The greatness of novels like *Sebastian Knight, Bend Sinister* and *Lolita* comes from a sense of unbearable pain somehow mastered through the resources of art and imagination, and these works exude a sympathy which is lacking in most of the Berlin novels and in the autobiographical sketches.

A HAPPY MAN

Sadly, at the end of his life, the very success of *Lolita* gave him the time and freedom from external pressures to revert to those mandarin postures which were always a temptation to him, and the last novels seem cold and sterile, strangely defensive for all their polish and brilliance.

Field's biography, written very much in collaboration with Nabokov, is a useful and interesting book. Field makes no attempt to be exhaustive; what he does rather is to make Nabokov more comprehensible to us by filling in the background. He describes the extensive Nabokov family — high bourgeoisie or lower aristocracy, with strong European and liberal tendencies. He paints a moving portrait of the artist's father, liberal diplomat and amateur lepidopterist, whose murder by right-wing fanatics in 1922 was surely as traumatic for Nabokov as exile.

He gives a fascinating account of the world of Russian *emigrés* in Berlin in the interwar years, when Nabokov kept himself and his family alive by giving lessons in tennis, boxing, English, French and prosody, and writing poems, stories, novels, cabaret sketches and even film scripts. The final chapter gives us a glimpse of Nabokov in America and especially of his relations with Edmund Wilson.

Nabokov emerges from all this as a reserved but, above all, a happy man. A man who went his own way, who never conformed, but who did not make a fetish of his nonconformity either. Of course, as Field is the first to acknowledge, the books and not the life are what is important. But, as with every major artist in our secular world, his life has an exemplary, almost a religious quality. This book does not tell us everything, but it tells us enough to make us pause and wonder at the miracle of art and human resilience.

NOTES

*Nabokov: His life in Part, Andrew Field, Hamish Hamilton, £8.50

16

A Sense of Waste *

The current vogue for literary biography surely needs an explanation. Any scholar who wants to make a quick name for himself, capture the main reviews, win the top literary prizes, even, probably, make enough money to re-roof his house — any such person is well-advised these days to find a suitable figure in (preferably recent) English literature and write his or her biography. I'm not sure when the vogue started. It wasn't particularly noticeable in the late 1950s and early 1960s. But now it is well and truly upon us. It is the *life of* Proust or Virginia Woolf or Faulkner, not their novels, that people want to read and talk about. Proust's biographer, flying in the face of everything *A la recherche* has to say, claims, when he arrives in France to promote his book: 'Qui connait *A la recherche* qui ne connait qu' *A la recherche*?' Meaning that we need the biography in order to make sense of the novel.

Few biographers make such absurd claims for their work. But though sophisticated readers may pay lip-service to the notion of intentional fallacy, the consensus of the literary establishment is that it is the lives rather than the works that we are all interested in. Yet it is almost fifty years since Sartre wrote *La Nausée*, which should have effectively put paid to the notion that it is possible to write meaningful biography at all; and Sartre was only taking up the point that Kierkegaard made a century and a half ago, that since life is lived forwards but recounted backwards, history and biography are never going to get at the truth.

But that of course is the rub. It is not the truth that people are after. The vogue of the classic novel clearly has much to do with precisely this, that people have a need for lives which are rounded, completed, seen as a whole, 'backwards'. Why they should have this need, and why it should have grown stronger in the seventeenth and eighteenth

A SENSE OF WASTE

centuries are questions best left to psychologists and historians. Perhaps it is that the less sense we can make of our own lives the more we need to read about the lives of others, to discover the kind of sense that exists there even in so tragically sense*less* a life as that of a Keats or an Owen. The surge of interest in biography in recent years may thus be related to the demise of the classic novel. For though 'well-made' novels still go on being reasonably well made it is impossible for the more intelligent and sensitive writers and members of the reading public to ignore the fact that they are an anachronism. The literary biography (in two volumes) thus neatly plugs the gap left by the disappearance of the three-decker novel.

Yet the matter is not as simple as Sartre and the New Criticis and the followers of Foucault would suggest. The idea that we can explain the work by the life is clearly nonsense; but so is the idea that there is *no* relation between the two. Sartre was right to argue that we should not live our lives as though they were biographies, but a good biography of a dead writer can give us something of immense value: the sense of the relations, between achievement and potential, between the art he created and his private life. A good literary biography usually ends by filling us with awe and wonder: awe at wasted potential (there is always waste) and wonder at what has been achieved (achievement is always miraculous).

But we have not yet come to an end of the contradictions. 'Of any poem written by someone else', Auden wrote in 'Dichtung und Wahrheit' ('An Unwritten Poem'), 'my first demand is that it be good (who wrote it is of secondary importance); of any poem written by myself, my first demand is that it be genuine.' Auden here reverses the point I have just made. It is the individual who must be conscious of motive and cause; the reader must simply respond to the work. Here Auden echoes Valéry's remark that he would rather have written a mediocre poem in full consciousness of what he was doing than a great poem in a fit of inspiration. For both of them the making of works of art is what dignifies and gives meaning to life; an artist's relation to his art must remain a moral one: there must be no cheating. But it would be absurd to ask the reader to think in such terms, since he would never know what constituted cheating in the first place.

The many wonderful poems Auden wrote about writers — Yeats, Voltaire, James, Rimbaud, Melville — testify to his continuing preoccupation with the mysterious and complex relations between a man's work and his life. But these are essays in imaginative reconstruction, not biographies. By and large Auden was against biographies of writers: 'They are always superfluous and usually in bad taste,' he claimed. Of course, 'the biography of an artist, if his life as a man was sufficiently interesting, is permissible, provided that the biographer and his readers realise that such an account throws no light whatsoever upon the artist's work'. Clearly he did not feel *his* life had been sufficiently interesting, and asked his friends to burn his letters after his death so as to make a biography impossible. On the other hand, as Carpenter points out in his thoughtful Preface, Auden insisted in print on a life of Pope because so many of Pope's poems grow out of specific events which need explaining, and of Hopkins because of his problematic relationship to his art; and he was himself a wonderful reviewer of other men's letters.

It is true that Auden's life wasn't particularly interesting (if by an interesting life we mean the life of someone like Napoleon or, at least, Gladstone); but Carpenter rightly believes that an account of it may throw light on the works and on a whole period of English literature. By Auden's criteria, too, the life does tell us a good deal about the nature of this odd thing, art, and of its role in our existence.

What Carpenter has done is to provide a careful and factual account of Auden's life; he is not afraid to discuss the poems and even to pass value-judgements, but he does this with modesty and restraint and without in the least giving the impression that he believes he has said the last word. Though the book has unfortunately been rather badly proof-read, and though there are a few factual errors and places where Carpenter does not seem to have fully understood the remarks he quotes, the impression by and large is of an unpretentious, workman-like volume. I cannot see that we shall need another life of Auden for a very long time.

For the first few chapters the adjective that kept occurring to me was 'useful' — here were details about who Auden knew at school, at Oxford, his links with the Group Theatre, and, most important of all, an account of exactly which poems were written when. (Carpenter more or less takes over Mendelson's views about the canon, but he is deft at plotting the development without being dogmatic when the evidence does not warrant it.) However, as I went on reading, I began to get carried along until, by the end, I felt I had read not just a useful but a moving, even a harrowing book. And the credit for this, though of course partly Carpenter's, is very largely Auden's.

What comes through is the man's enormous hunger, a kind of huge

A SENSE OF WASTE

gaping hole needing desperately to be filled — with the writing of poetry, with sex, ultimately with affection and love. Carpenter quotes Auden's remark, apropos Ackerley's *My Father and Myself*, that if we are going to talk about our sexual preferences we shouldn't stop short of detail: 'Frank as he is, Mr. Ackerley is never quite explicit about what he really preferred to do in bed. The omission is important because all "abnormal" sex acts are rites of symbolic magic, and one can only properly understand the actual personal relation if one knows the symbolic role each expects the other to play.' Auden's favoured mode of sex, it seems, was fellatio, and Carpenter elsewhere quotes his dismissive remark about his heavy smoking: 'Insufficient weaning. I must have something to suck.' Carpenter is too sensible to try and draw large conclusions from this, but he leaves us to ponder whether that gaping emptiness with its desperate need for oral satisfaction produced both the poetry — the speaking voice in the poetry, we might even add — and the insatiable search for sexual satisfaction. I say too sensible because to press such a connection and to try and explain it in terms of any particular theory, psychoanalytic or otherwise, would inevitably rouse in us the feeling that there were at least half a dozen other equally convincing explanations. There probably are no single explanations, but there is no doubt that there are connections.

Neither the production of poetry nor the smoking of cigarettes nor the practice of oral sex was clearly enough. 1939 is a watershed in Auden's life. His phenomenally precocious development depended, we can see, looking back, on his sense that if he trusted his luck and kept going, sooner or later he would find Atlantis. His sense, so powerfully expressed in the early poetry, that he must get away from England if he was to survive, that 'England, this country of ours where nobody is well' would stifle him if he stayed — this had led to his sojourn in Berlin, his journeys to Iceland, China, America. It had also been one of the main causes of his popularity. There are writers like that, whose struggle with their private demon strikes a chord in a whole generation. Perhaps it is because in their egocentricity they see their own personal crises in terms of the body politic. Auden, we can see from this biography, was a Romantic poet in the sense that he wrote poetry in direct reaction to personal joys and despairs. Yet the idiom in which he wrote (and he was rather like Graham Greene in this) evokes not a private world but the England of the time — or at least an image of it which many people seem to have found convincing.

THE MIRROR OF CRITICISM

It was not, in the end, because of the state of the nation, but because of his personal need for a haven which was not England, that Auden finally decided to emigrate to America. He was thirty-two and already a famous poet. He had been in New York only a few months when he met Chester Kallman, a student at Brooklyn College, and some fifteen years his junior. According to Carpenter, Kallman deliberately set out to seduce Auden. Within weeks Auden was deeply in love. He seems to have suddenly felt that at last he had reached that Atlantis for which he had only half-consciously longed in the past few years. 'Of course I know that Love is a fever that does not last,' he wrote to his close friend, Mrs Dodds, the wife of the classical scholar E. R. Dodds, 'but for some years now I've known that the one thing I really needed was marriage, and I think I have enough experience and judgement to know that this relationship is going to be marriage with all its boredoms and rewards.'

The euphoria lasted barely two years. In that time Auden wrote, lectured, and returned to the religion of his childhood. Then came the crash. Kallman took a lover, told Auden that sexual relations between them were at an end. Auden's world crumbled, and my feeling is, though Carpenter does not make this explicit, that he was never really able to put it together again.

This does not mean that the poetry declined. Carpenter is of the opinion, and I agree with him, that the view of Auden as a great poet in his twenties who threw away his talent in later life is nonsense. His work is of a piece, and, if anything, there are more fine poems after 1941 than before. Unlike Carson McCullers, with whom Auden briefly shared that famous house in Brooklyn Heights (Britten and Pears were also lodgers, but left in disgust at the squalor), he did not collapse completely, hit the bottle and give up writing. On the contrary, he became more and more strict with himself, kept to a frighteningly tight schedule which involved going to bed very early and getting up at six-thirty to work. But this, one feels, became more and more an imposition of the super-ego, something he was doing to keep himself going rather than anything he really relished doing. The days of wonderful insouciance which had given birth to the *Letter to Lord Byron* were gone for good. The intrusion of Kallman into his life and the crisis this had precipitated left him permanently weak and vulnerable, only too aware that what he wanted above sex and fame was a home and a companion. Carpenter recounts his attempt at an affair with a young woman, and in later life he went on asking women to marry him, the last being Hannah Arendt, who had just lost her husband and sweetly rebuffed him.

That is why the book is so desperately sad. Auden's start was so marvellous that the end is all the more shocking. He remained a poet of wonderful gifts, and a friend whose eccentricities people were prepared to put up with for the sake of his humanity and wit. But he was drinking more and more heavily, relying on drugs to keep him going, and on other drugs to help him sleep. He was becoming more and more dogmatic too, repeating the same stories again and again, paying no attention to anyone else. The last days at Christ Church make harrowing reading, and death must have come as a blessed relief.

Curiously, the relationship with Kallman held to the end, and the younger man died within a year of Auden's own death, saying that he'd 'lost his criterion', a strange phrase Carpenter does not try to elucidate. Though Carpenter is as objective as he can be, he clearly, like so many of Auden's friends, thinks the relationship was a disaster. Kallman comes through as weak, vain and selfish, using his ties with Auden to advance a mediocre poetic talent and making no bones about his need for a continual supply of beautiful young men. Yet he clearly gave Auden something that none of his English or European boyfriends could give him, and if Auden went along with the relationship to the end it was because he needed it — and who can say if what he needed was self-destruction or marital comfort?

There is a passage in the opening section of *The Orators* (written in 1931, when Auden was twenty-four), which is prophetic. The prizeday speech turns on the question of those who are guilty of excessive love:

> Then the excessive lovers of their neighbours. Dare-devils of the soul, living dangerously upon their nerves. A rich man taking the fastest train for the worst quarters of eastern cities; a private schoolmistress in a provincial town, watching the lights go out in another wing, immensely passionate. You will not be surprised to learn that they are both heavy smokers.... You can call them selfish, but no, they care immensely, far too much. They're beginning to go faster. Have you never noticed in them the gradual abdication of central in favour of peripheral control? What if the tiniest stimulus should provoke the full, the shattering response, not just then but all the time? It isn't going to stop unless you stop it. Daring them like that

only makes them worse. Try inviting them down in the holidays to a calm house. You can do most for them in the summer. They need love.

Carpenter does not try to explain why Auden needed love so much. He does not insist on the relationship with his mother, which seems to have been strange enough, or even raise the question of whether Auden's aggressive openness about his sexual tastes might not have sprung from a deep sense of guilt about them. Yet I think that no one reading this biography could fail to be struck by such questions.

Carpenter tells the story of Auden as a young man going for a walk in the country with a friend. Suddenly Auden realised that he had lost three pound notes. 'Never mind,' he said, 'we will pick them up on the way back.' 'Four hours later,' Carpenter writes, 'in the dusk, as they returned along the ridgeway, they saw three notes fluttering in the grass. Auden picked them up and put them back in his pocket without a word.' Later, when he and Isherwood were in China, 'covering' the Sino-Japanese war, Isherwood wrote to Spender that Auden 'knows he won't be killed, because Nanny would never allow it.' And in one of his very last poems, 'A Lullaby', Auden wrote:

> Let your last thinks all be thanks:
> praise your parents who gave you
> a Super-Ego of strength
> that saves you so much bother...

But was Auden right? Was not his insistence on the power of his super-ego not itself suspect? One wonders whether the miracle of the early poetry and the ease with which he imposed himself on the literary establishment, like the ease with which he seems to have found sex whenever he wanted it — was this not felt by him deep down as something for which he was sooner or later going to be punished?

In later life he seems to have tried to forestall that insistent question by seeing himself as a kind of holy sinner, a man who has to go to the bottom of degradation to show that even here redemption is possible. Some of his most beautiful poetry has to do with such notions as these, as in the central stanzas of 'Atlantis' (1941):

> If, later, you run aground
>   Among the headlands of Thrace
> Where with torches all night long
>   A naked barbaric race

A SENSE OF WASTE

>   Leaps frenziedly to the sound
>   Of conch and dissonant gong;
>   On that stony savage shore
>   Strip off your clothes and dance, for
>   Unless you are capable
>   Of forgetting completely
>   About Atlantis, you will
>   Never finish your journey.
>
>   Again, should you come to gay
>   Carthage or Corinth, take part
>   In their endless gaiety;
>   And if in some bar a tart,
>   As she strokes your hair, should say
>   'This is Atlantis, dearie,'
>   Listen with attentiveness
>   To her life-story: unless
>   You become acquainted now
>   With each refuge that tries to
>   Counterfeit Atlantis, how
>   Will you recognise the true?

But here there is a curious kind of internal contradiction: to say: you must forget completely about Atlantis, you must listen with true attentiveness to the Siren's story, is perhaps to state a profound truth. But, stated, it becomes something else. The poet who says: I am humble, I am a holy sinner, and so on, is at once felt to be a charlatan. The fact is that Auden always longed for Atlantis, for a world where all contradictions would be resolved, and he was prepared to lose his life to find it. Yet he knew this was a neurotic longing, knew intellectually just what kind of a sin and just what kind of a psychological error it was. But of course this did not stop him longing — for who knows what primal frustration was in need of appeasement?

This is not simply a matter of the life. It also affects the poetry. Was Auden not too successful too easily? Eliot at least saw the danger. 'His predictions for Auden's future', Harry Levin recalled, 'virtually constituted a laying on of hands. Yet he hinted at one slight caveat against the hazards of facility.' Just because poetry came so easily to Auden he tended to underrate it. Clearly he would have been happier as a court bard or at least as a court poet like Dunbar. But in this century that could not be. And one feels that because he never encountered any genuine difficulty in his poetry, because he never came to the point of feeling both the need to sing and the impossibility of singing — a feeling experienced probably by all the great writers of the century — poetry was unable to support him in a time of crisis. Maybe by now we are tired of the high value set on art by a Rilke, a Kafka, a Joyce — that all-or-nothing sense we get from their work. Certainly Auden helped English poets to realise that one could be a fine and a modern poet without this desperate view of art. But such 'realism' is double-edged. A Kafka, a Beckett, an Eliot, made their art out of the simultaneous awareness of its value and of its total lack of value: art was the proof that Atlantis was a mocking mirage; Auden's relegation of art to the statute of a 'secondary world' left him pathetically vulnerable as he searched for salvation in the primary world. There is a kind of dignity in the lives as well as the works of Kafka and Beckett and Eliot which is sadly lacking in Auden, an acceptance of failure and sacrifice, of life's inevitable refusal to come up to our expectations of it, which Auden, for all his protestations to the contrary, never achieved.

Carpenter, at the end, forsakes his usual reasonableness, and goes for the large claim: 'A re-reading of Auden's poetry, through all its decades and in all its many versions', he writes, 'shows how right Lincoln Kirstein is to place him "with Picasso in painting, Stravinsky in music; a master of the uses of our whole past, projected into the present and prophesying the future".' That master was not Auden; it was Eliot. For Auden did not do what Eliot and Stravinsky and Picasso did: invent forms for our time and endow them with the authority of total authenticity. He inhabited the forms of the past, brilliantly, humanely, renewing their possibilities. Yet his voice is rarely quite his own, the echoes of Yeats and Eliot haunt his verse, the poetry shifts from music-hall to high rhetoric without the two ever quite blending, as nursery jingle and ritual lament do in Stravinsky, as childish doodle and classicism do in Picasso. Of him it could not be said as he said of Eliot:

> When things began to happen to our favourite spot,
> a key missing, a library bust defaced,
>   then on the tennis-court one morning,
>   outrageous, the bloody corpse, and always
> blank day after day, the unheard-of draught, it was you
> who, not speechless from shock but finding the right

A SENSE OF WASTE

> language for thirst and fear, did much to
> prevent a panic...

It could not be said of Auden, but of course it took Auden to say it of Eliot, so movingly, so simply, so precisely. 'Your sixty years have not been wasted', he ends the birthday tribute to the older poet; and no one who has any interest in poetry or in the English language would be foolish enough to say that Auden's sixty-seven had been wasted either. Yet even here there is something slightly too knowing about the understatement, as though Auden were himself just a little too aware of the felicity of that final phrase. After reading Carpenter's biography one does feel sadness at a kind of waste. But I suppose we should be grateful for what we have.

NOTES

*W. H. Auden: A Biography, Humphrey Carpenter, Allen & Unwin, 1981

17

The Heart of the Matter*

Graham Greene will be seventy-two this year, and he has been publishing novels for over fifty years. *The Man Within* came out in 1929, in the same decade as *The Waste Land, Ulysses* and *The Magic Mountain*. Like nearly all his subsequent novels it has been filmed and translated into umpteen languages. I remember seeing the film in a small open-air cinema in Egypt when I was ten or eleven. *The Human Factor*, published two years ago, gave no sign that Greene was out of touch or out-of-date; indeed, his particular form of the spy novel, which grows out of Dostoievsky and Conrad, seems to become more topical and 'true to life' every day. And this is not just a matter of skilful adaptation to the times. Greene has always had an uncanny instinct for what is about to happen, and why — whether it be in Cuba, Haiti or St James's. *The Quiet American* is still the best book about the American involvement in Vietnam, yet it came out not in 1975 or even 1965, but in 1955.

By any criteria then, a remarkable achievement: to have been popular for so long, to have reached a global audience, yet always to have written out of conviction and according to his own high standards. From *Stamboul Train* (1932) on, Greene's novels show a rich awareness of political issues, a profound exploration of the interaction of public and private, and a continuing struggle to articulate the fundamental questions of faith and the meaning of life. Could one ask more of any writer?

Surely not. And yet — though easy to read, even compulsive, yet never trivial — Greene's novels finally disappoint. Somehow, he turns aside at the crucial point, evades the issue. It is difficult to be precise, but in everything he writes there is a sense of compulsions insufficiently acknowledged, a reliance on novelettish and journalistic clichés, a sense, finally, of an overriding sentimentality. This is, of course, what

THE HEART OF THE MATTER

makes him so popular. The English in particular can never have enough of Scott Fitzgerald, Jean Rhys and other sentimental and self-pitying writers. On the other hand, Beckett will never find a home in the hearts of the English novel-reading public, yet his themes (failure, the impossible struggle for salvation) are after all very similar to Greene's, and can alert us to what Greene lacks — that quality of exhilaration conveyed by even the grimmest of great art, whether it be *Lear* or *Molloy*. Compared to his great contemporaries — Borges, Beckett, Malamud, Bellow, Golding, Spark, Robbe-Grillet — there is in Greene's work a depressing quality of monotonous repetition, the sense both of his own awareness of failure and his inability to do anything about it.

In a splendid essay on A. E. W. Mason, Greene remarks:

> Unfortunately he had the modesty of a good fellow rather than the pride of the artist, and he rated himself too low. Yeats decided to 'dine at journey's end with Landor and with Donne': in the celestial club Mason would not have seated himself higher than the author of *The Dolly Dialogues* or Quiller-Couch. It is as if his journey into success, social and financial, had not allowed him time for thought, thought about the techniques of his profession, thought even about its values.

This is an excellent point: it is too often forgotten that the targets an artist aims at largely determine what he produces. But then, since Greene himself makes the point, surely it is odd to accuse him of the same mistake? It is clear, too, from the diary he kept while writing *A Burnt-Out Case*, and from the *Collected Essays*, that Greene is a highly conscious and intelligent artist, as concerned with the problems of his craft as his masters James and Conrad.

Yet even the *Collected Essays* suggest precisely the kinds of confusions and uncertainties which mar his fiction:

> Of course I should be interested to hear that a new novel by Mr E. M. Forster was going to appear this Spring, but I could never compare that mild expectation of civilised pleasure with the missed heartbeat, the appalled glee I felt when I found on a library shelf a novel by Rider Haggard, Percy Westerman, Captain Brereton or Stanley Weyman which I had not read before.

The essay in which this remark appears, 'The Lost Childhood', is similar to Proust's meditations on the power and urgency of childhood reading. The difference is Proust's recognition that our relation to the world and to books changes — that for an adult book to touch us as one or two special books did in childhood, it must impinge on us in quite new and unexpected ways. Proust then devoted his life to discovering those ways.

For Greene, though, there is a radical division in the heart of experience itself: there is the missed heartbeat and the appalled glee of childhood reading; on the other hand, the 'civilised pleasure' of adult reading. Understandably, the latter does not offer many temptations to the man or the writer; yet he cannot ignore the limitations of a Rider Haggard, a Stanley Weyman. Nevertheless, the urge to recapture the much more real pleasures and terrors of childhood colours all he writes. Scobie, almost at the end of his tether in *The Heart of the Matter*, has a dream:

> That night he dreamed that he was in a boat drifting down just such an underground river as his boyhood hero Allan Quatermain had taken towards the lost city of Milosis. But Quatermain had companions while he was alone, for you couldn't count the dead body on the stretcher as a companion.

Greene's heroes try to live again the adventure stories of their childhood, but succeed only by leaving their companions behind and finding not buried treasure, or the witch Gagool, but simply their own deaths. That, however, is treasure enough.

Anything but the worst is a dangerous temptation; when the worst comes we can sigh with relief, for we know that we have reached rock bottom and can fall no further. That is the basic Greene paradigm. Thus Scobie, 'swerving the car to avoid a dead pye-dog', asks himself, 'Why do I love this place so much? Is it because here human nature hasn't had time to disguise itself?' But even that is a dangerous illusion; we never reach the hard rock; there is still disguise and deceit. Scobie is embroiled in both through his own pity and humanity. He knows very well the dangers of pity, the way it brings lies and evasions in its wake, but he is powerless to help himself.

The power of *The Heart of the Matter* comes from a curious ambivalence on Greene's part. Scobie is aware of what he is doing, and he judges it quite accurately: 'They had been corrupted by money and he had been corrupted by sentiment. Sentiment was the more dangerous, because you couldn't name its price.' The Church, however, is not swayed by such weaknesses, and it naturally condemns Scobie; he has no option (once he finds he cannot give up either his mistress or his belief in the teachings of the Church) but to condemn himself to perpetual damnation by suicide.

Yet Greene will not let it rest there. He wants us to feel that Scobie is a good man, the best there is — better certainly than his wife, or his mistress, or the spy Wilson, or any of the unfeeling colonials or wily Syrians with whom he has to deal. Greene spares nothing to convince us: he gives Scobie a dead daughter whom he loved; he makes Helen Rolt an unthinking little fool, and his wife a nagging bore; he makes Scobie heroic in his vain attempts to allay his wife's pain by concealing his suicide. As a result of all this we are caught in the same sweet destructive syrup as Scobie — aware of the correctness of the Church's attitude (he must give up his mistress) but deeply sympathetic to his human feelings:

> The responsibility as well as the guilt was his — he was not a Bagster: he knew what he was about.... He felt tired by all the lies he would some time have to tell; he felt the wounds of those victims who had not yet bled.

Jane Austen wrote to her sister during the Peninsula War: 'How horrible it is to have so many people killed! — and what a blessing that one cares for none of them!' Surely a worthy sentiment, though perhaps not one that our liberal age would approve of. It is the kind of sentiment we expect from Waugh or Spark, but Greene is not that kind of Catholic. He wants to have the best of both worlds, and, like the addict who cherishes his addiction though recognising its consequences, he is locked in a self-destructive spiral. For each of his heroes is seen — and sees himself — as a victim. The victim, usually, of the naïve, the young, the innocent. 'God preserve us from the innocent,' remarks the narrator of *The Quiet American*, and he could be talking of the child of 'The Basement Room', Helen Rolt, Marie Rycker and all the others, as well as Alden Pyle and Americans in general.

For these are the destroyers with a clean conscience, who imagine they can get out of the lies and complications of adult life by passing the buck or living by the book. The heroes, on the other hand (from Dr Czinner in *Stamboul Train* to the protagonist of *The Human Factor* forty-six years later) accept that death is the only way to get rid of the burden of guilt and evasion. 'From childhood I have never believed in permanence, and yet I had longed for it,' says the hard-boiled journalist narrator of *The Quiet American*. 'Always I was afraid of losing happiness. This month, next year.... If not next year, in three years. Death was the only absolute value in my world. Lose life and one would lose nothing again for ever.' But this view of life is deeply sentimental because it suggests that there is, behind the evasions, a clarity, a simplicity, a Truth — that we can, somehow, return to the world of Rider Haggard and John Buchan. 'I ran towards the finish just like a coward runs towards the enemy and wins a medal. I wanted to get death over.' Even as he speaks, he betrays what he says. The language, the striking phrase, gives the game away. Greene wants to present us with reticent, desperate heroes, who have reached rock bottom in order to leave behind forever the world of hypocrisy and doubt; they then find that they have to go further, the whole way to death in fact. But the language gets in the way: to say 'the heart of the matter' is to find myself on the periphery again.

Kafka wrote in his diary:

> Have never understood how it is possible for almost everyone who writes to objectify his sufferings in the very midst of undergoing them. Thus I, for example, in the midst of my unhappiness, sit down and write to someone: I am unhappy.... And it is not a lie, and it does not still my pain; it is simply a merciful surplus of strength at a moment when suffering has raked me to the bottom of my being and plainly exhausted all my strength. But then what kind of a surplus is it?

This is a central paradox of the novel. Kafka has not of course tried to resolve or explain it, for he knows instinctively that no resolution is possible. He is content to point to the problem in all its mystery. For the novel, from its origins in Puritan diary-keeping and soul-searching, has always been intimately bound up with the idea of sincerity, with escape from the conventions of art and the direct reporting of life 'as it really is'. But to write down 'I am unhappy' is to transform it into something else.

Most novelists are untroubled by this: a few sense it and try to ignore it; even fewer, more concerned with truth perhaps than their fellows, face up to it. Greene's theology often strikes one as so Calvinist precisely because he is caught in the double-bind of the sincere man protesting his sincerity, of the humble man proclaiming his humility. He writes to get to the heart of the matter, yet the act of writing carries him back into the world of hypocrisy and ambiguity to escape from which he had written in the first place.

THE HEART OF THE MATTER

That Greene is uneasily aware of some deep contradiction involved in the very act of writing can be seen by looking at an episode in *Stamboul Train*. Dr Czinner, the socialist revolutionary returning to his country to take part in an uprising, but learning that he is too late, feels a deep sense of relief at the news. Like all the Greene heroes, the sense of his inevitable impending death brings him a measure of peace he had not known in his life of exile and disguise. But he is still troubled. He approaches an Anglican priest also travelling on the train: ' "I wished to speak to you," he said, "of confession." At the sound of the words he was momentarily young again.' A popular novelist joins them:

'We really have here the elements of a most interesting discussion,' said Mr. Opie. 'The doctor, the clergyman and the writer.'

Dr. Czinner said slowly: 'Have you not left out the penitent?'

Mr. Savory said: 'In a way surely *I* am the penitent, in so far as the novel is founded on the author's experience, the novelist is making a confession to the public. This puts the public in the position of the priest and the analyst.'

Mr. Opie countered him with a smile. 'But your novel is a confession only in so far as a dream is a confession. The Freudian censor intervenes.'

Dr Czinner stumbles away from them. He has not come here for a discussion of confession, but for something infinitely more important: to confess.

And this is the problem. Greene sees that the novelist is the servant of the public and of his inner censor; he must develop his plots and maintain a level of verisimilitude, when what he wants all the time is to utter the necessary words and reeive the blessed absolution. The more sincere he tries to be, the more he is then caught up in the confusions of rhetoric. Proust and Kafka faced up to this and made their fiction out of their disillusionment with the novel; Greene, on the other hand, clings to the classic form of the novel as Scobie clings to his adultery: he can do nothing else.

All this is made very plain in Greene's most 'confessional' book, *A Burnt-Out Case*. The way in which the novel is an instrument of exploration but also the ultimate betrayer, and Greene's mixture of love and hatred for it, all emerge clearly here. Querry, a famous Catholic architect, has come to Africa to escape from the failure of his faith in his art or his religion. He has reached the end of the road, and is content to stop where the ship stops, at the leper colony, and spend the rest of his life there, doing whatever is required of him.

The opening, as the still anonymous passenger is ferried up-river towards the *leproserie*, is superb in its explosive reticence. But very quickly Grene spoils what he has achieved: 'If he had been a murderer escaping from justice, no one would have had the curiosity to probe his secret wound.' Greene cannot avoid pressing his point home, nor can he resist the rhetorical flourish. But a secret wound becomes something else when described. Greene simply cannot resolve the technical problem of how to convey Querry's emptiness without falsification. Later he writes: 'He nearly added: "That is my trouble."' Greene, of course, does add it, and he goes on adding all the time. He even uses that cheapest of novelistic devices by having Querry dream and say in his dream: 'I am sorry, I am too far gone, I can't feel at all, I am a leper.'

So the sentimentality creeps back in, until even the title starts to seem too pat, betraying what it says in the process of saying it. Eventually Greene is forced even to provide a banal plot to show how Querry is sucked back into the complexities of life, and to lead him to his inevitable death. Even here he cannot leave well alone, and, as in *The Heart of the Matter*, he tries to touch us: Was Querry a saint or a sinner? The reader feels a momentary glow, for, after all, it is possible that he too is better than he thinks he is, that he too may perhaps be saved.

The curious thing is that Greene is aware of his temptations: 'Am I going too far from the original vague idea: am I beginning to plot, to succumb to the abiding temptation to tell a good story?' he asks in his working diary. Yet he cannot help succumbing, for he cannot conceive of writing a novel in any other way. One has only to compare *A Burnt-Out Case* with a masterpiece like Robbe-Grillet's *La Jalousie* (another novel of repressed feelings, possible adultery, and the search for the meaning of life in a densely-forested colonial setting) to see what a major writer could make of it all. 'Perhaps I am not accepting the reality but struggling against it,' Greene notes, 'and at the same time I am frightened of what the doctor calls "sentimental", which is his word for picturesque or dramatic.' In the end, *A Burnt-Out Case*, from its title through to its conclusion, is sentimental, picturesque and dramatic, and not the one thing he wanted it to be — 'real'. Robbe-Grillet, eschewing the picturesque and the dramatic, conveys the real all right, yet even if Greene could see this, one doesn't feel he would abandon his own way of working. I am guilty, he would say, and run towards the finish.

Dr. Fischer of Geneva is very different from the other novels, but the same contradictions plague it. It is, in fact, not a novel at all but a novella or long short story. This is not just a matter of size: *Moderato Cantabile* and *Not to Disturb* are probably shorter, but they are novels, dealing as they do with the interplay of character and event. This, though, is a work whose point is not the characters or 'reality', but merely the recounting of an anecdote.

The story is told in the first person by an Englishman in his fifties, who has lost a hand in the Blitz and now works for a chocolate firm in Geneva as a translator. Dr Fischer is one of the richest men in Geneva, a parvenu who has made his fortune through the invention and marketing of a brand of toothpaste. His daughter, a pure virgin of twenty, falls in love with the narrator, they marry, and she dies in a skiing accident. Dr Fischer has the odious habit of giving dinner-parties at which the guests are humiliated by having to eat whatever is put in front of them, and then rewarded with expensive presents. A regular group, all very rich themselves, they go on enduring the humiliation in order to pick something up for nothing. The narrator attends two of these parties, the second in a mood of desperation after his wife's death, and it is with this second party that the book is mainly concerned.

For here Dr Fischer plays his last card: he places cheques for 2,000,000 Swiss francs in crackers. He then asks the guests to help themselves. The only hitch is that one of the crackers contains not a cheque but a bomb which will almost certainly kill the unfortunate person who happens to choose it. All but one of the guests succumb, and in a final twist, the suicidal narrator buys back with his 2,000,000 francs the last cracker, which must, by a process of elimination, contain the bomb.

He joyfully pulls it, only to discover that Dr Fischer has won the last round, for there is no bomb there either — Dr Fischer has robbed him of his own death. After the final humiliation, the host walks away from the guests and shoots himself.

Can anything at all be said for this farrago of nonsense? The dedication is already something of a warning: 'To my daughter Caroline Bourget, at whose Christmas table at Jongny this story first came to me.' Greene has always admired Stevenson and James, and the dedication places the tale firmly in the nineteenth-century tradition of story-telling, confident of the world it purports to describe and of its public reception. The first sentence confirms this: 'I think that I used to detest Doctor Fischer more than any other man I have known just as I loved his daughter more than any other woman'. Hate, love, 'more than any other' — here is that nineteenth-century confidence in attributing motive and emotions which has more or less vanished from the art tradition of fiction, although it still thrives in the underworld of children's stories, thrillers, and teenage romances.

From then on the book gets worse and worse. Greene has never been good on love between the sexes, and his story of the love that unites the beautiful, virginal, mature and intelligent daughter of Dr Fischer and the pathetic narrator never even begins to achieve a sense of reality. In fact all the people in the book are so one-dimensional and at the same time to unpleasant that only an exceptionally gripping story could make one persevere. Not only is the story not gripping, it positively drags, and even Greene's famous images are no help: 'I could feel the fumes of their hostility projected at me like tear-gas...'; 'hate like a raincloud hung over the room...'; 'eyes like polished chips...' the tired images are trotted out, but it all seems terribly mechanical, almost — but is that possible? — deliberately bad.

Is there any explanation for this? The narrator has the familiar feeling: that happiness cannot last; that death would be a relief. But the book is much more clearly about Fischer: much is made of his God-like or Satanic power. He himself insists that, unlike the greed of his rich guests, his greed is 'like God's'. God wants to humiliate men, we are told, and so does Fischer. Is this then an allegory, that last resort of the desperate novelist? It seems to me that, as always, the problems of religion and of narration reflect one another. For if Fischer is like God, he is also like the novelist as Greene conceives of him — tempting the public, humiliating them, knowing they will always come back for more. He cannot ever forgive them for not acting the confessor, refusing absolution. Like Querry, he hungers for some essential, rock-like truth, the heart of the matter, but gets adulation instead. I am not a good man, I am bad, he cries, and they smother his cry with praise of his honesty, his genius, his saintliness.

The aged Dr Fischer has no friends, only toadies; in the end there is nothing else for him to do but shoot himself. Greene seems to be trying to send across some self-critical message. Yet he has only himself to blame for the low esteem in which he holds the art he practises. Kafka

THE HEART OF THE MATTER

and Proust came to the point where they no longer had any confidence in fiction, but they transformed that lack of confidence into the basis for a new form of fiction. Greene has never taken that step. He remains bound to his own contradictions and confusions. Yet even so it is not a bad art; his work is much more interesting than that of Anthony Powell or of most of his younger English contemporaries. But it is a sad art because one thinks how much better it could have been. Or could it?

Could Scobie have changed? Was it not a sign of his honesty and humanity that he did not? He was honest with himself, we say, and profoundly human in his sympathy, which is more than those around him were. But fatally sentimental. Fatally sentimental.

NOTES

*Graham Greene, *Doctor Fischer of Geneva or The Bomb Party*, Bodley Head, £4.50

18

Body and Mind*

> ━━━━━▶●●━●●◀━━━━━

I first came across the name of Borges in Maurice Blanchot's *Le Livre à venir*. That was in 1959, in the narrow corridor that linked the main shop to the foreign books department in the old Parker's, across the road from Blackwell's, in Oxford. In that corridor were stacked all the books that wouldn't fit into any of the usual categories, and there, crouching between the shelves, I read about the Aleph, about Shakespeare who 'resembled all men in everything save in this, that he resembled all men', and about the mysterious Pierre Menard who saw it as his life's work to reproduce word for word two chapters of *Don Quixote*.

In Paris later that year I picked up a copy of the French translation of *Ficciones* in the ugly yellow cover in which the NRF condemn their South American translations to face the world, and read it through in one afternoon. Borges, it turned out, had that rare quality, shared by Proust and Eliot, of being unputdownable. Also, he was *my* author. No one, as far as I could tell, had heard of him in England, and very few people in France. In 1961, however, all that changed. In that year Borges and Beckett were named joint-winners of the Formentor Prize, perhaps the only time that a literary prize has gone to absolutely the right people.

With the award of the Formentor Prize, Borges's international reputation was established. Throughout the 1960s his fame spread across the world, and a flood of translations appeared in English.[1] And not only was everyone suddenly reading Borges, everyone was quoting him. It became almost impossible to open a book on social theory or psychoanalysis or intellectual history, particularly in France, without finding it preceded by an epigraph taken from Borges. And so idiosyncratic yet so impersonal was his style that by the late 1960s we had the feeling that Borges had always been with us; it became impossible to conceive of a world in which his work did not exist. As a result today we have come to take him for granted, much as we take Beckett for granted and as we took Nabokov for granted in his last years. For all three men seem to belong to another world, the world of the great modernists, of Joyce and Eliot and Kafka, a world where quality and not quantity are the determining factors and where reticence rather than aggressive confession is the norm. Yet in all three there is the sense of a new modesty, as if after the heroic efforts of the great modernists the inevitable limitations of art — and of life — had been recognised and, however reluctantly, accepted.

International success is surely almost as dangerous to a writer as total neglect. Few writers in our century have been able to shrug it off and go on with their chosen work unaffected by publicity and the inevitable growth in self-consciousness it brings with it. Beckett has been one of the few, but Nabokov, I felt, suffered — or rather, his art suffered. With Borges it has been a little different. Recognising, as he has recently said with a characteristic blend of modesty and irony, that by now there are many people who can turn out the sort of thing that made him famous much more brilliantly than he ever could himself, he has had to cast around for something else. All those stories of labyrinths and endless libraries, all the traps and sleights-of-hand of a multi-faceted baroque style — these he has reluctantly put aside and tried, in his last two collections, *Dr. Brodie's Report* and *The Book of Sand*, to create something simpler yet equally striking. The themes are still to some extent the same, but the emphasis has shifted from the book that is read to the tale that is told, from the library to the bar where, out of the hubub of general conversation rises the voice of one man, a man with a particular tale to tell. And his models, he informs us in his prefaces, are now quite specifically Kipling and Stevenson and Wells. It is his ambition, it seems, to write as simply and as directly as them.

Is Borges serious? we ask. Or is this one more trap laid for the unwary reader by the master of camouflage? Of course the distinction serious / ironic is too simple, though we often use these terms as if they divided the world of artistic tone between them in much the same way as the kings of Spain and Portugal once divided the geographical world. But in relation to Borges there are a number of points that have to be borne in mind. He has, for one thing, always stressed his admiration for English literature — a literature full of people, he is fond of saying, not books, like that of France or Germany. And he has always gone for those English writers who seem least in fashion: de

Quincey, Morris, Chesterton, Browning. Partly, of course, his tongue is in his cheek. It is all too easy to refer to Eliot or Kafka; better to shock and surprise by pointing out the virtues of the unfamiliar. Partly it may be the curious effect of reading books which belong to a culture other than one's own in a different way from the people within that culture: the Poe of Baudelaire and Mallarmé is not the Poe of an American or an English writer; just so the Kipling or Wells of a Latin American, however cosmopolitan, is clearly different from that of an Englishman. Partly too it has to do with Borges's old-world quality, the sense we get of his belonging to a world of dignity and restraint, a world of ordered values and social stability, a world where the term 'liberal intellectual' still means something, which links him with Nabokov and distinguishes him sharply from Joyce and Kafka. But finally I think that what draws him to these writers, and now in his old age more than ever, is their essential *innocence*.

Borges's love of Kipling, Stevenson and Wells, it seems to me, stems from the same source as his love of Old English and Icelandic culture. In the ancient epic writers, as in the writers of the twilight of the British Empire, there is a sense of utter self-confidence; there are no doubts about the nature of the art they practise or the reactions of their audience. This makes for a kind of lightness, a speed and clarity which are very attractive.

The trouble with innocence, however, is that it cannot really be striven for. Much as a modern writer might like to create stories as Kipling or Wells did, he simply cannot do so, especially if he has, in the past, written stories like 'Averroes' Search' or 'The Garden of Forking Paths'. I also wonder whether he really needs to. I can see the temptation of Kipling and Wells, but there is really no comparison between their often trivial and unreal anecdotes and the depth and richness of a Borges story.

Where, precisely, does this depth and richness lie? Well, for one thing, Borges is often very funny. 'Pierre Menard' is a superb satire on the small world of symbolist coteries which effortlessly catches the interplay of sentimentalism, Fascism and decadent Catholicism that characterised them, even though all this is incidental to the main, mind-boggling point of the story: that it is all too easy to write tales and novels; that what is hard, and therefore interesting, is to rewrite, *word for word*, something that in its inception was as open and free-wheeling as *Don Quixote*. But of course nothing is incidental in a Borges story, and another point that emerges is that genius can spring up in the most unlikely places, or that what from one point of view might be regarded as crankiness can be seen from another as genius. Throughout this story, as in the others collected in *Fictions* and *The Aleph* and written in the 1940s, what is so dazzling is the richness of invention in little space, the continuing surprises as Borges works the different registers of language and convention. 'The Garden of Forking Paths' is a good example. It is not simply a fine idea translated into a short story but a continuing play on the possibilities and inertias built into language, built into the notion of 'murder story', 'spy story' and, quite simply, 'story'.

But that is not all. When we think of Borges, we inevitably think of labyrinthine temples, fantastic libraries which reduplicate themselves endlessly in time and space, men who merge into one another with bewildering ease. But if that is the substance of Borge's world, it is only created in order that it might finally be negated. That is, Borges's central subject has always been not the labyrinth of the world, not the infinite multiplication of the self, but, on the contrary, the search for the meaningful space and the unique individual. 'Tlön, Uqbar, Orbis Tertius' is devoted to the description of a universe governed entirely by the laws of the imagination. But that story ends: 'Then English and French and mere Spanish will disappear from the globe. Then the world will be Tlön. I pay no attention to all this and go on revising, in the still days at the Adrogué hotel, an uncertain Quevedian translation (which I do not intend to publish) of Browne's *Urn Burial*.' And in 'The Garden of Forking Paths' the protagonist muses: 'In spite of my dead father, in spite of having been a child in the symmetrical garden of Hai Feng, was I — now — going to die? Then I reflected that everything happens to a man precisely, precisely *now*.'

How to bring to consciousness the unique moment, the uniqueness of the self? For the unique is, strictly speaking, unimaginable. And this is both torment and relief. Torment because we can never quite see ourselves as the singular beings we are, fulfilling our singular destinies in irreversible time, and therefore always remain at a remove from our bodies; relief because in this way we do not have to face up to our own mortality. Death, which brings a man's uniqueness home to him in the moment of taking it away, is the flame round which the majority of Borges's stories hover. Sometimes his meditations are quite explicit: 'In time there was a day that extinguished the last eyes to see Christ; the battle of Junin and the love of Helen died with the death of a man. What will die with me when I die...?'

THE MIRROR OF CRITICISM

In the face of death the poet has no special privilege. Dante, dying in Ravenna, is 'as unjustified and as lonely as any other man', and Marini's final revelation is merely that 'the high and splendid volumes which, in the shadows of his chamber gave out a golden glow, were not (as his vanity had dreamt) a mirror of the world, but one more object added to the world.' Indeed, the paradoxes of human life are heightened for the writer. He is caught in a double-bind, for on the one hand there is the urge to speak, to make sense of life, his life in particular, and on the other there is the awareness that to speak is only to multiply shadows, to evade the singular. His weapon is the imagination, but imagination is also the enemy. That is why the protagonist of 'The Garden of Forking Paths' can convey *his* message only at a fearful cost: 'He knew my problem was to indicate (through the uproar of the war) the city called Albert, and that I had found no other means to do so than to kill a man of that name. He does not know (no one can know) my unnumerable contrition and weariness.'

The sending of a message, the creation of pattern, implies the killing of what was alive. The urge to write must be submitted to, but the guilt cannot be evaded. This is ironically brought out in 'Death and the Compass' where a private detective, Lönnrot, is fooled by a criminal who recognises Lönnrot's penchant for what is interesting (i.e. patterned) as opposed to what is merely possible (i.e. arbitrary) and deliberately creates an 'interesting' plot which leads Lönnrot to his death.

In such ways Borges brings to the surface the essential guilt of the writer and in so doing points to that reality which can never be uttered. Like Wallace Stevens he recognises that there is a continuing dialectic between self and other, imagination and reality, and that art must never falsify by implying that there is a final 'truth'. 'The other one, the one called Borges, is the one things happen to,' begins the parable called 'Borges and I'; and it ends with the devastating line: 'I do not know which of us has written this page.' For if it is the awareness of death which brings about an awareness of uniqueness, then it is possible for the writer to create multiple little deaths, so to speak, in the course of his work. The unique self is a permanent exile, forced to flee every refuge, every home: it can only be caught in motion. That is why the greatest of the stories toss us restlessly from the labyrinth of infinity to the prison of the self, and why the perpetual shifts of the baroque style force us at every turn to adjust and readjust and readjust again.

The paradoxes of man's infinite imagination and finite body are perhaps most bitterly and savagely caught in the story called 'The Theologians', where the heresiarch Euphorbus, consigned to the flames, says: '"This has happened and will happen again.... You are not lighting a pyre, you are lighting a labyrinth of flames. If all the fires I have been were gathered together here, they would not fit on earth and the angels would be blinded. I have said this many times." Then he cried out, because the flames had reached him.'

One could say of Borges's recent stories, as well as of all his poetry, that the flames have never reached them. Borges, of course, was a poet before he was a writer of stories, but though his poems have often been moving meditations on his central themes, they have hardly been embodiments of the paradox in the way the stories have. This has to do with the fact, I think, that poetry has to be based on some kind of prior agreement between writer and reader; the solid ground it rests on are the facts of rhyme and rhythm and metre. Eliot's extraordinary achievement was due in large measure to the way he was able to dissolve this ground and yet always retain the sense of its imminent presence, but this was an exceptional feat, and anyway poetry in the romance languages is always more likely to retain allegiance to *a concept of poetry*. The selection from Borges's last two volumes of verse now brought together in *The Gold of the Tigers* seems to me to maintain the admirable middling quality of the earlier poems. But what has now happened is that the prose has taken on the same characteristics. The fire has gone out and we are left only with the multiple worlds of the imagination.

For example 'The Congress', which Borges in his preface singles out as the finest piece in *The Book of Sand*, is a variation on the theme sketched out in a single page in an earlier volume under the title 'The Rigours of Science'. 'The Congress' is not really long enough, at twenty pages, to develop character, but it is too long for the single point it is making. Moreover, the surface realism only throws into relief the unlikeliness of the whole anecdote. Again, 'Avelino Arredondo' has much in common with the earlier 'The Waiting'. Both are about men alone, in hiding, waiting. But where the hero of the earlier story has betrayed his comrades and is waiting for them to catch up with him, Avelino is a self-appointed political murderer who is being careful not to implicate anyone else in his deed. Consequently, there is a deep sense of rightness at the end of the earlier story which is missing from the latter. For in 'The Waiting' the hero has dreamt many times that the men he has betrayed have caught up with him and are about to kill him, and when this does finally seem to happen we feel that even if it still is only a dream this no longer matters: he is suffering his punishment in his own hell. Avelino carries through his deed with a somnambulistic precision, but the story remains an intriguing anecdote and no more.

In the earlier stories, as I have said, the guilt is exorcised in the act of writing and the act of imagination itself is finally tracked down and revealed as the prime culprit. In the recent stories, as in the poems, the act of story-telling is never questioned. Now this is quite natural in an oral culture, where the bard has a specific function and a necessary role; but there is something slightly false in a writer today adopting that position. We feel uneasy, and this unease is reinforced by the prefaces Borges has recently taken to adding to his works. In *The Book of Sand*, for example, he writes: 'At my age (I was born in 1899) I cannot promise — I cannot even promise myself — more than these few variations on favourite themes. As everyone knows, this is the classic recourse of irreparable monotony.' Here we are being presented with the image of The Writer as Stoic. It is an image Borges employs so frequently that we have come to think of it almost as his trademark. But if one compares this with the image of the writer presented in 'Borges and I' or in the closing lines of 'Tlön, Uqbar, Orbis Tertius' quoted above, one sees what has been lost. The parable and the story overstress ever so slightly ('an uncertain Quevedian translation'), and so convey an ironic distance: such a view of himself by the narrator is seen as both an ideal and as a temptation. But such ironic self-consciousness is missing from the prefaces.

It would be a pity if Borges were to accept unquestionably any image of himself, he who has so wittily and brilliantly shown up the folly of ever accepting oneself as just this or just that. And yet, having said this, one is bound to add that there are many wonderful things in both these books. I particularly like his elegy to the German language, and the man of the future who in one of the stories remarks: 'I remember having read, not without pleasure, two tales of imaginative literature.... Travels of a Captain Lemuel Gulliver, which many people take to be true, and the *Summa Theologiae*.' Borges is still one of the most readable and thought-provoking writers we have ever had.

BODY AND MIND

NOTES

The Book of Sand, Jorge Luis Borges, trans. Norman Thomas di Giovanni, E. P. Dutton, $7.95

The Gold of the Tigers: Selected Later Poems, Jorge Luis Borges, trans. Alastair Reid, E. P. Dutton (bilingual edn), $3.95 (paper)

1 As far as I can see an almost total chaos reigns in the world of Borges translations and editions in English. It is difficult to buy two books by Borges which do not reduplicate at least one item. When are the publishers going to bring some order into this situation?

19

The Ethics of Silence*

When Eliot was asked what he thought of Hugh Kenner's book about him, *The Invisible Poet*, he replied: 'I like the title.' If any major writer of our time has been even more invisible than Eliot it is Samuel Beckett. Ever since the runaway success of *Waiting for Godot* in 1953, Beckett seems to have taken the place of Picasso as the symbol of what is most exciting and most hateful (depending on the point of view) about modern art. In the last fifteen years his work has been pored over by students and written about by professors, but it has contrived, like Eliot's poetry, to remain untouched by this activity. And as far as his life is concerned, though there have of course been plenty of rumours, and anecdotes keep drifting back, Beckett's shyness, his steadfast refusal to give interviews, his aversion to publicity, have succeeded in shielding him from the public gaze. Though this is understandable and even admirable, it has meant that there are not only many gaps in our knowledge of such things as the genesis of his works, but also that it has been hard for us to see the larger patterns of his writing. All this has now been made good by Deirdre Bair in a biography that is not only painstaking and thorough, but also profoundly moving.

Richard Ellmann has attacked Ms Bair in a carping article in the *New York Review of Books* for failing to have any general theory about Beckett's work or its relation to his life, and therefore for lacking in focus. In fact this is precisely the book's strength. Unlike so many biographers she does not try to explain the work by the life; she is content to record what has happened and to let the material speak for itself. Of course she must have shaped it, but she has done so with such understanding and discretion that the portrait that emerges is, to my mind, utterly convincing. This seems to me to be the authentic portrait of a very great writer and a good man.

Beckett was born in 1906 in the fashionable Dublin suburb of

THE ETHICS OF SILENCE

Foxrock. His father was a building contractor who had left school at fifteen to enter the family firm, was a keen sportsman and a *bon viveur*. His mother, whose family regarded itself as much more genteel than the Becketts, was a woman of iron determination, upright, Puritanical and withdrawn, though fond of animals. Both Beckett and his elder brother were gifted sportsmen and did well at school before going on to Trinity College, Dublin. But where Frank was submissive and ready to follow the path marked out for him by his family, Sam was like his mother, seemingly determined to go his own way.

By his third year at Trinity his interest in sport (he captained his school at rugby and cricket and toured England with the Trinity cricket team) had given way to more intellectual pursuits, and his Professor of French began to see in him a possible recruit to the faculty. In 1928 he went to Paris as the Trinity *lecteur* at the Ecole Normale Superieure, and here he met Joyce and his circle through Tom McGreevey, who was to be a lifelong friend and the only correspondent to whom Beckett ever opened his heart. (Ms Bair has had access to the three hundred or so letters Beckett wrote to McGreevey before his death in 1967, and frequently quotes from them.) In Paris Beckett began to write in earnest, but his family preferred to ignore the copies of *Whoroscope* and *Proust* which he sent home. When he returned to Dublin to take up a probationary teaching appointment at Trinity he seemed to have a promising career ahead of him as teacher and writer, but life rarely works out in these comfortable ways. In 1930 and 1931 a whole range of psychosomatic illnesses began to manifest themselves: cysts, boils, headaches, insomnia. By the end of November 1931 a crisis had been reached: 'He had taken to his bed permanently, lying rigidly in the foetal position facing the wall. He lowered the blinds and spent days in darkness with the blankets pulled over his head. Nothing and no one could get him to move.' The breakdown was kept quiet, and Beckett was sent to relatives in Kassel to recover. From there he wired the University and tendered his resignation.

The next six years seem to stretch out forever in an ever-increasing nightmare, as Beckett and his mother lock in a struggle of wills. Without enough money to survive in Paris, since his parents saw no reason to support him and publishers seemed uninterested in his work, yet unwilling to take any of the jobs his parents and ex-teachers tried to obtain for him, Beckett drifted into a state of depression, illness and despair. He seemed to take a perverse pleasure in outraging his mother, was rude to friends, drank heavily, let his appearance go, got into fights. Periodically he escaped — to London, where he underwent analysis at the Tavistock Clinic, wrote *Murphy*, and was wretchedly miserable; to Germany on walking holidays or tours of the art galleries — but there was a doomed, self-destructive quality to all his actions, as though the struggle were not simply between himself and the outside world, but between parts of himself, and that victory for either side would be equally fatal.

In the middle of this his father died, and his mother grew even more obsessed with observing the proprieties, horrifying her son by the show of love and devotion she put on to the memory of a man for whom she seemed to have had nothing short of contempt in his lifetime. When Frank married and moved out the nightmare reached its nadir. Finally it seems that both Beckett and his mother must have sensed that to go on as they were would rapidly destroy them both. In the last weeks of 1937 he packed his bags and finally left for Paris. He wrote to McGreevey: 'I am what her savage loving has made me, and it is good that one of us should accept that finally as it has been all the time.'

Within days of his arrival his agent wrote that *Murphy* had been accepted — by the *forty-third* publisher to whom it had been sent! Beckett resumed his old friendships and even started seeing Joyce again, but now events were moving fast. In 1938, as he was coming home late one night, Beckett was stabbed in the street and almost killed. A woman who was passing by took immediate charge and got him to hospital. Her name was Suzanne Deschevaux-Dumesnil, and she was seven years older than Beckett. When he was discharged she moved in with him, and they have lived together ever since.

At once the war was upon them, and they found themselves caught up in Resistance work, first in Paris and then, when their cell was betrayed, escaping to the village of Roussillon in the Vaucluse. Here Beckett had another breakdown, brought on by the enforced solitude and the sense of guilt at the death of so many of his friends at the hands of the Nazis while he, once again, had got away. To stay sane he began to work on a new novel, *Watt*. But when the war ended and they were able to return to Paris, the familiar pattern started to repeat itself: publishers wanted tales of heroism; Beckett, as he told a friend, was only interested in failure.

However, the war had wrought a decisive change in him. He had begun to write in French, recognising that he was through with Dublin and London forever; and the continuing rejections had finally made him indifferent to publication. While Suzanne sewed to keep

THE ETHICS OF SILENCE

them alive, Beckett shut himself up and wrote. Between 1946 and 1949 he wroter *Mercier and Camier*, *Molloy*, *Malone Dies*, took four months off to write *Waiting for Godot*, and finished off with *The Unnameable*. In her spare time Suzanne had been hawking his MSS round publishers and theatres. Suddenly, in 1950, within a few months of each other, Jerome Lindon accepted the Trilogy for Editions de Minuit, and Roger Blin decided to take a chance on *Godot*. In between, his mother died.

The rest of the story is, in a sense, a sort of giant appendix. By the end of 1953 *Godot* had brought Beckett the fame that had been denied him for twenty-five years; in 1954 his brother died; in 1961 he was awarded the Formentor Prize with Borges, and in 1969 the Nobel Prize. Now he was so busy with translating his own work from English into French, French into English, both into German; with overseeing his plays whenever he could; with being polite to visiting scholars, old friends and young admirers, that the problem became how to find time for the prose fiction he felt to be his main task. In recent years it would seem he has grown less anguished by his failure to produce anything on the scale of the trilogy; his works, after all, may be getting shorter and shorter, but they are hardly getting slighter. At past seventy he is still writing with that willingness to take risks and that refusal ever to repeat a past success which we are used to in painters and composers at the end of their lives, but which is hardly ever found in writers.

The picture that emerges from this beautiful and moving book is that of a man who all his life has valued one thing above all others: his independence. He has never for a moment given up the struggle to remain free amidst the manifold temptations of our century to give up that freedom. But what is extraordinary about him is the way he has carried that struggle into literature itself. Early on he wrote about the absurdity of Balzac's characters, those 'clockwork cabbages' who would never dream of suicide. His own early hero, Belacqua, asks nothing better than to stay put. For to move in any direction, in writing as in life, is to lose your freedom, to submit to the meaningless banality of social or novelistic or even grammatical convention. 'The ideal game for Beckett', Ms Bair says, describing the chess game in *Murphy*, 'was the one in which none of the pieces was moved, for from the very first move, failure and loss were inevitable.' As soon as he has begun to speak Beckett seems to recognise the pattern into which his utterance will fall, and hurriedly dissociates himself from it. This gives

THE MIRROR OF CRITICISM

an extreme density to his writing, for he moves in the course of one sentence through three or four different registers. But it also results, in the early work, in a feeling of terrible frustration and constriction. The drama which was being acted out in the years 1930 to 1945 finds its mirror in the writing itself, which is split down the middle and locked in a destructive battle with itself. In 1946, however, comes a moment of positively Proustian revelation. One night, by the sea in Dublin, while visiting his mother, Beckett was overcome with the sense that 'the dark he had struggled to keep under' was the real source of his work. 'I can now accept this dark side as the commanding side of my personality,' he said later. 'In accepting it, I will make it work for me.'

Writing thus became a way not of reflecting life or of escaping from life, but of retaining balance, a mode of exploration in the twilit world between beginning and end. It is to Ms Bair's credit that she manages to convey this without in any way overstressing it and thus turning it into one more banality. She is occasionally naïve, and her interpretations of individual works are sometimes wrong. The proof-reading, too, has not been what it might be with this book: a date is wrong on p. 406, a footnote is missing on p. 684, and there's a howler on p. 698. But these are small blemishes in a book that succeeds triumphantly in conveying the sense of the infinitely complex relationship between life and art and of the essential interaction of the two. 'I couldn't have done it otherwise,' she ends by quoting Beckett as telling her. 'Gone on, I mean. I could not have gone through the awful wretched mess of life without having left a stain upon the silence.'

NOTES

*Samuel Beckett: A Biography, Deirdre Bair, Jonathan Cape, £8.50

20

A Modern Poet *

Until I read this collection of Donald Davie's essays I had never realised the urgency of his poetic quest. Of course urgency by itself is no proof of quality, but without it there can be no development, no real achievement.

Davie started as a member of the 'Movement', that reaction to the apocalypticism of the 1940s which, ably led by poets such as Larkin and Amis, swept all before it in the 1950s. One of the earliest essays in this volume, dated 1954, finds him pleading for a recognition of the value of the occasional poem, and in the title essay, written a year later, he insists with pride that he views his own poetry as strictly *minor*. Like Larkin and Amis he sensed that there was an urgent need for a poetry which would recognise precisely its own limitations. But of course while one may long for poems which 'could be complete in themselves', poems which 'can be walked round' as so many eighteenth-century poems are, Davie was too well read a poet not to realise that such poetry cannot be written today. Eighteenth-century poetry depends on tone, it gains its strength from consensus, from agreement about the rules that operate in society as well as in literature, and today all such consensus has gone. The problem for the modern poet is 'not that he has no mythology to use, but that he has no one such mythology, in other words, that he has too many mythologies to choose among and nothing to direct him which one to choose in any given case'. Davie may have started with Larkin and Amis, but he soon came to see the insular smugness of their stance. Pound and his American followers, on the other hand, though liberating him from a Little Englander attitude, were quickly recognised by Davie as accepting the values of modernism a little too easily: their lack of awareness of the losses involved have come to seem to Davie to smack of a dangerous innocence. It is simply not possible to get rid of rhetoric, to ransack at will the imaginary museum of other ages and other cultures and to write out what one feels straight from the heart. The 'shadow of the rhetorician's dishonesty' as Davie puts it in his brilliant and highly critical essay on Lowell, cannot simply be wished away, it must be accommodated. But how?

There is no answer to this question. What we see is the poet Davie driven from position to position, unable to close his eyes to the contradictions of any for very long, yet unwilling to plunge into the kind of radical doubt that lies at the heart of the work of a Rilke or an Eliot. He wants very much to say: 'This is only a poem, a small thing, though good enough in its way', but when he does this he recognises a very English smugness creeping back in, and when he tries to cope with that by acknowledging it, it merely reintroduces the smugness at a further remove. Hence his recent attempts at writing long poems, as though he hoped in the process to find a voice, a form. This, to my mind, was a mistake. He lacks Auden's commitment to dialectic and Auden's wit, and as a result poems like the 'Six Epistles to Eva Hesse', while no doubt amusing to write, are tedious to read. The title poem in the present volume, which is also the longest, seems to me, for similar reasons, to be a failure. There is no progression: each new section merely repeats and fills out what was said in the opening section, and in the process inevitably dilutes it. And, naturally enough, Davie finds it hard to discover a note to end on, and opts for the least convincing, a throw-away phrase that is far too predictable.

A number of the poems in this volume, though no more than a page in length, suffer from the same defects. But an even greater number overcome these triumphantly, and in the process convey a sense of something quite new and very powerful. Take 'Gemona-del-Friuli, 1961-1976'. The innocent dates hide two tragedies, one personal, the other public. But this is not something we need to know beforehand, and the poem leads us into it with deceptive gentleness:

> We have written to Giulia, saying
> 'Are you still alive?'
> And no reply comes.
> This is a bad lookout.

Fifteen years before, in that same place, the poet had faced a personal loss, but had managed to come to terms with it:

> That was the place;

A MODERN POET

> Where a calamity, not
> In any case undeserved,
> Chastened, I thought, and instructed
> Gravely, biddable me
> As to the proper proportions
> Of the dead to the living, of death
> To life...

But now an earthquake has hit the region, flattening in a moment the town that had stood for 700 years:

> What colour of justification,
> What nice, austere proportion
> Now can be put on the mountains?
> At whose hands this chastisement?

This is nothing less than Job's question, and how many poets alive today could cope with it like that? The poetry recognises its own inevitable limits and the coolness of language and rhythm, the compression which is simply a heightening of the easy speaking voice with which the poem opens — all this brings home to us as nothing else could the *unimaginableness* of disaster, the utter otherness of the world.

Other poems in this collection, notably 'The Harrow' and 'Widowers', convey an even greater sense of wonder, understanding and controlled power. Davie's compression results not in wit but in the emitting of a kind of blow that forces one to catch one's breath. It is a remarkable achievement.

And it is the result, I am convinced, of his continuous questioning of his craft and of its place and function in our lives, which is so strikingly exhibited in the volume of critical essays. To take in the arguments of that volume fully, to follow up its many leads, is to grasp not just where poetry is going at the present time, but what it is that poetry has always tried to do. It seems to me that it does for the poetry of the last thirty years what Eliot's *Selected Essays* did for the years 1900-30. This is a large claim, and I make it with some hesitation. But in both cases what comes through most strongly is the writer's feeling of responsibility — to language, to poetry, to his fellow men. Davie's praise of poets as diverse as Tomlinson, Sisson and Bunting is not proof of an indiscriminate eclecticism but proof rather that for the man who is alive to poetry and not out to prove a theory — of life, of art — the world is full of surprises, the human spirit richer and more varied in its manifestations than one could ever *imagine*. It is this same combination of a questioning intellect and a readiness to be open to experience which has led to the rich vein of poetry — the surprisingly rich vein of poetry — so evident in *In the Stopping Train*.

NOTES

The Poet in the Imaginary Museum: Essays of Two Decades, Donald Davie, ed. Barry Alpert, Carcanet, £6.00

In the Stopping Train and Other Poems, Donald Davie, Carcanet, £2.00

21

On the Brink of Parable*

A cat has nine lives, but how many has a man? William Dubin, a fifty-eight-year-old biographer, married, with two grown children, living out in the country, falls in love with a girl less than half his age. Fanny Blick enters his consciousness when, out on his daily jog, pondering the D. H. Lawrence biography he is about to embark on, she stops to ask the way. He notes the firm body, face verging on the beautiful, dark hairs on her chin, Star of David dangling from her neck, and, when she drives on, berates himself: 'Ah, Dubin, you meet a pretty girl on the road and are braced to hop on a horse in pursuit of youth.' She reappears as part-time charlady and Dubin finds it hard to concentrate with her in the house. In his study one day she throws off her clothes and flings her panties at him. The biographer throws them right back: No, Fanny, not in my wife's house. He thinks he has lost her but they meet again, fix a *rendez-vous* in New York. He waits but she doesn't turn up, later claims she lost the address and agrees to go with him to Venice. Once there, with poor Dubin on fire, she over-eats, falls ill, and then, when he is out scouring Venice for his erring daughter (whom he thinks he's seen with a man his own age), she invites a gondolier into the room and Dubin returns to find them at it on the floor. Suitably chastened and embarrassed, he goes back to his wife — how could he make such a fool of himself? But it's a terrible winter, and his work comes to a standstill. He pushes, wills himself into activity, a better relationship with his wife — nothing. Then Fanny re-enters his life, they become lovers, and he begins to burgeon, physically and mentally. But now Fanny starts urging him to divorce and, when he does nothing, vanishes. Another terrible period of acedia descends on him: he is impotent with his wife, she half-heartedly takes a lover, the Lawrence book comes to a stop again. But Fanny reappears, buys a farm in the neighbourhood, and we leave Dubin with the recognition

THE MIRROR OF CRITICISM

that he, who had always thought of himself as a truthful man, will have to revise that option, and with Fanny suggesting he spend half the week with her, half with his wife. Who knows, perhaps he will. A simple enough story to summarise, but nothing in Malamud is ever what it seems to be. Or rather, it is that, and then it is another thing, and still another. The mind and eye, dazzled by so much surface, long for a little depth. And so does Dubin. To have an affair with a girl his daughter's age is a foolish and undignified thing to do, a pathetic attempt to live another life, and it brings in its wake all the humiliations such behaviour has traditionally called down on foolish and lecherous old men. But it is also a coming alive for someone who has begun to die on his feet, and, for the biographer of D. H. Lawrence, a spur to major achievement, real understanding of his subject. Is Dubin then wrong to start the affair? To persist with it? Is he wrong not to leave his wife? Not to make a clean break and start where love and youth await him?

Back from Venice he turns fiercely to his exercises, his dieting, his work: 'He had once more to be the man he'd been.' But who was that man? A writer of obituaries, he had drifted into the writing of lives. It's a way of getting to know yourself: you see in others who you are. But couldn't one equally say that to write the lives of others is to fail to live your own? 'Everybody's life is mine unlived. One writes lives he can't live. To live forever is a human hunger.'

To ask such questions implies that there are answers. The novel guides us into the much more frightening region where we begin to wonder if there really ever are any answers to the questions we may put to life. Dubin is essentially a lonely man, a Jew without faith, but with strong memories of both his parents, his resigned waiter father (how lovingly Dubin plays on the ambiguities of his father's profession), and his mother, who went mad and killed herself when his elder brother drowned. He has met his wife in peculiar circumstances, which both bind them close and keep them apart: she was a widow, looking for a father for her child, decides to put an ad in the paper; Dubin, working for the paper for which her ad was destined, sees it and knows his fate. They meet and decide to try and make a go of it. It is a choice, and he has never regretted it, though she has her fads and he never quite ceases to feel he is a substitute for her dead husband. Her son, a Vietnam deserter, has holed up in Scandinavia; their daughter is a drop-out with her own amorous problems to which she does not admit her parents. Dubin is sensitive enough to be able to distinguish

146

greatness and fraudulence, but without the drive and self-centred energy of his subjects, Lincoln, Thoreau, Lawrence. Lying on his bed alone, he wonders if he is lonely. Would be be better off all by himself? Yet he too is a waiter; he will wait and see. Meantime, he tries to cleanse his system of the detritus and falsity which one accumulates in the course of the weak compromises of life, and to get the Lawrence book off the ground. Throughout the perishing winter he never lets up on his jogging, walking, press-ups, bicycling exercises, dieting and the rest. His wife begs him to relax, swears it is doing him no good; but Dubin goes on willing himself back into condition, into hope, into a belief in himself.

But will is not enough.

Once, he says, the future was the next biography. Now it is old age. Reading this novel one realises how quickly other novels usually hurry through people's lives, and how, in this essential respect, they flatter and comfort. *Dubin's Lives* gives us, as no other book I know (with the exception of the last part of Chaucer's *Troilus and Criseyde* perhaps) the terrible sense of human frustration, of time hanging heavy and no way forward. The poets of course have spoken about this, and other artists in journals and letters have let slip cries of anguish. Dubin notes some of these: Coleridge's 'A grief without a pang, void, dark and drear'; St Augustine's: 'I wind round and round in my present memories the spirals of my errors'; Chekhov's 'Why is it so dull here? It is snowing, a blizzard, there is a draft from the windows, the stove is sizzling hot, I had the thought of writing, and am not writing anything.' Life seems suddenly without a point or perhaps it does have a point and its name is Fanny Blick? Who knows? Certainly not Dubin.

Perhaps then it is our notion of life being this thing or that thing which has to give way. Maud, the daughter, comes home and confesses she's 'fed up with my ego.... I want an end to confusion and pain. I'd like to be a different person than I've been.' 'My child,' Dubin says, 'take your clear luminous eyes in your hand, as my father used to say, and look through them to see life clearly. In life fulfil yourself.' But who is Dubin to talk? It's all very well for him to say: 'You've always called yourself a Jew. Jews live in the world. Don't hide from pain, insult, fear or failure. Don't expect perpetual serenity. It's not that kind of life or real world.' But does Dubin know what life is or how each of us should live his life, be himself?

The Jewish element hangs lightly over the book and it too is subject to the same ambiguous interpretations as everything else. From

THE MIRROR OF CRITICISM

Fanny's New York apartment Dubin can look down into a synagogue and see old men praying: is that fulfilment or the opposite? His Jewishness forces Dubin to feel uneasy with both the hedonistic life and the ascetic. It is like a pebble that halts the stream a little, makes him press a little harder against the current of life. The stream flows on, but in some indefinable way this attitude gives Dublin a depth, a quality, which eludes the more dashing heroes of life and literature. Malamud achieves this remarkable feat through a use of language which itself acts as a sort of pebble, just deflecting the natural flow of English: 'She had shed deep mourning, but mourning lingered where it knew the ground'; 'if you dared look, you earned seeing'; 'If I have any eloquence, with him I lose it.' The slight but insistent foreign — Yiddish? — rhythms give the language a supple, living quality, transform pain and frustration into pleasure.

And this is Malamud's triumph. For much is at stake, not just for Dubin but for Dubin's own biographer. The passage in which Dubin recalls his discovery of his vocation — writing Berryman's obituary: 'The dead poet was terribly real. He felt an imperious need to state his sorrow, understanding, pity — wanted with all his heart to preserve the man from extinction' — that passage, though undercut later by Dubin's doubts, survives them all. You can't relight lives, but you can recreate them. What Malamud does so amazingly here is to convey the sense that whatever you do you will live your life, that there is no possibility of radical change or blinding illumination — but also that a central element in our lives is our longing for understanding, for a sense of what our own lives essentially are. The book ends with a list of Dubin's works. We see from it that he did indeed finish the Lawrence book, and went on to write two more: *The Art of Biography* (of course); and *Anna Freud* (with Maud D. Ferrera). Now Anna was Freud's Antigone, and who else can this Maud be but Dubin's own errant daughter, now obviously become his Antigone? We close the book meditating on the strange pattern of human life. But are we right in our guess? Perhaps that Maud is someone else altogether, a second wife, a prim research assistant, and we have simply fallen into the old trap of patterning, ordering, where there is only randomness, one random event and then another.

But there is another explanation. Perhaps it is not Dubin's biographer who writes the list, but Dubin himself, in a moment of wishful thinking as he doodles helplessly with his Lawrence notes. Suddenly, much else falls into place. Perhaps it was all day-dreaming,

ON THE BRINK OF PARABLE

from the very first meeting with Fanny, and this helps to explain the coincidences, unlikely episodes, the insistent parallel between Fanny and Maud? And then we see that we must really ask: If it was 'real', was it any less of a dream? And with this question we come, I think, to the heart of the book. In all Malamud's fiction there is this haunting feeling that life is about to reveal itself, to take on the quality of parable, but it never quite does so. Or is that, perhaps, the parable? How real is reality? Can we not make it more real? The answer is, we can't — but also: books like this one, do. It is Malamud's finest achievement to date, a wonderful novel.

NOTES

*Dubin's Lives, Bernard Malamud, Chatto & Windus, £5.95

22

A Triumphant Return*

'Doukipudonktan, se demanda Gabriel excédé' is the famous opening sentence of Queneau's *Zazie dans le métro*. The trick is to repeat the opening 'word' out loud again and again until one suddenly realises what it is one is saying. When that happens one finds oneself laughing despite oneself, though why exactly one should do so is as difficult a question to answer as any of the other questions about the causes of laughter. Obviously it has something to do with the arbitrary nature of written signs in our languages, and with the fact that conventions of orthography are both necessary and absurd, as are the conventions of written narrative. In *Djinn* a little girl gives the narrator a lesson in the telling of stories. She asks him for a 'story of love and science fiction', and when he obliges by beginning: 'A robot meets a young lady,' she immediately stops him: 'You don't know how to tell stories. A real story is always told in the past tense.' He tries again: 'A robot met a — ' But this is still wrong: 'Mais non, pas ce passé-là. Une histoire, ça doit être au passé historique. Ou bien personne ne sait que c'est une histoire.' The narrator thinks for a moment, then launches into his story once again: 'Autrefois, il y a bien longtemps, dans le beau royaume de France, un robot très intelligent, bien que strictement metallique, rencontra dans un bal, à la cour, une jeune et jolie dame de la noblesse. Ils dansèrent ensemble. Il lui dit des choses galantes. Elle rougit. Il s'excusa.'

This is Robbe-Grillet's funniest and lightest novel so far. He is taking on Calvino at his own game, but the overtones of menace and darkness are still present. The narrator enters a deserted hangar at the appointed time, makes out in the gloom a man standing waiting for him: 'Monsieur Jean, je présume? Mon nom est Boris. Je viens pour l'annonce.' This is the coded message he has been told to give. But the figure answers: 'Ne prononcez pas Jean, mais *Djinn*. Je suis

A TRIUMPHANT RETURN

Americaine.' So it's not a man but a woman: the conventions of spelling and thriller plots have misled him. However, a moment later he discovers that 'she' is not a woman either but a tailor's dummy, animated only by the power of his imagination, and her husky voice issues not through her unmoving lips but from a sound system wired into the derelict building. He moves away in disgust only to be met by another dummy, identical to the first but this time she turns out to be real — or at least as real as anyone ever is in the pages of a book. For it may be that the narrator is imagining all this, the beautiful American girl, the whole bizarre world of Russian spies and an international ecological anti-machine movement into which he is drawn. We do in fact learn later that the narrator, Simon Lecoeur, is much given to fantasising. But is he even called Simon Lecoeur? He gave his name as Boris, but this was the code, and though after his disappearance a French passport in the name of Boris Koershimen is found in his flat, the police think it's a fake. At the American school of the rue de Passy where he teaches he is inscribed as 'Robin Körsimos, dit Simon Lecoeur', but his students call him Yann, spelt Jan.

The preface, where this information is given — shades of Nabokov and Borges here — only multiplies the hypotheses about his name and origins. It also directs our attention to the fact that the story of Simon and 'Djinn' which follows, was found on Simon's desk, ninety-nine neatly typed pages, divided into eight chapters of gradually increasing length and linguistic complexity. Eight weeks is the length of an American term, and so what we have here may not be either fiction or fantasy, but only a graded reader for students of French.

A comparison with Butor may be helpful here. Butor too would have organised his material in a rigorous way so as to exhaust the possibilities inherent in his material and in his initial decisions. But for him that would have been enough: symmetries and patterns are, for Butor, sufficiently satisfying in themselves. For Robbe-Grillet, however, they only represent what has got to be worked through if that which forever eludes definition is finally to be pinned down. Is not the educational character of the story merely one further lure? 'Derrière cet alibi, doit se cacher autre chose. Mais quoi?'

That, of course, has always been Robbe-Grillet's question, but in his recent novels the sense that narrative, as opposed to life, was free to do anything, quickly left the reader with the feeling that everything the narrative did was equally *un*interesting. But that is not at all the impression given by this novel. This is partly due to the irony and humour, which hint at a real desperation. Partly too it is due to the fact that when, as here, Robbe-Grillet does not make the erotic and the sadistic the central subjects of his work he taps unexpected resources in himself. That is partly why *Dans le labyrinthe* is the best of his early novels, the one in which the universal nature of his essential themes is most fully realised. And here too, in the episodes with the two children — more than half the book — we are in the realm of myth, not science fiction or strip cartoon. Those pages are perhaps not quite as good as *Zazie* itself, but much better than *Le Grand Meaulnes*. At one point Simon, for some reason he cannot even explain to himself, playing at being blind, eyes firmly shut, dark glasses on, a white stick in his hand, is led down endless alleyways by the little boy Jean (not Djinn). He could easily open his eyes, yet chooses not to. Why? 'Je dois avoir un sacré complexe d'Oedipe', he thinks to himself, and it is of *Oedipus at Colonus*, not the banalisations of Freud, that the scene reminds us — not of Roy Lichstenstein but of the great Picasso etching of the little girl, a light in one hand, leading the blind minotaur by the other.

The artist is both innocent child and blind master. He eliminates one or other at his peril. For too long — since *Dans le labyrinthe* in fact — Robbe-Grillet has tried to argue and to write as if art were merely a game. Of course it is not simply the imitation of reality; but it is also mystery, the confrontation of the unknown, unspoken. *Djinn* suggests a new humility in its author, a recognition of the fact that he may not hold all the cards. It is a pleasure to see a major artist finding himself once more.

NOTES

**Djinn: Un trou rouge entre les pavés disjoints*, Alain Robbe-Grillet, Editions de Minuit, 1981, 30F

23

The Really Real *

What Saul Bellow has been doing since *Herzog* is developing his own quite unique kind of novel. Like Virginia Woolf (he wouldn't thank me for the comparison) he has gradually discovered a form of fiction in which plot counts for extremely little, but which is open enough to include almost everything. Of course Bellow's minimal plots are very different from Virgina Woolf's: instead of house-parties and village fêtes there are divorces, court cases, deaths. The setting is urban, usually Chicago, which is seen as the archetypal modern city, and the cast includes hoodlums, media men, academics and politicians. The 'almost everything' also differs from Virginia Woolf's, for it includes all the horrors of slums and big cities, the senseless rapes and muggings and killings, the greed for fame and money, and the unspeakable monstrosities that go on in the whole world. Bellow wants to get Bokassa and his jewels as well as Idi Amin; Guatemala as well as Czechoslovakia; Vietnam as well as Auschwitz into his books. They must be nothing less than a long hard look at the whole of our civilisation as it stands, or totters, now.

Some might admire the ambition, others, more cannily, recognise its dangers. For who is Saul Bellow to tell us how we live and how we should live? Why should we listen to him rather than to another? This is where fiction comes in. Bellow's speeches *in propria persona* are often no more than the public airing of prejudice; a book like *To Jerusalem and Back* leaves us predominantly with a sense of the author's bigotry and arrogance. But in fiction all that is changed. Bellow, half-aware of the problem, never gives the impression in his novels that what is being said about the state of the world is being said by himself, or is to be taken as the final truth on the matter. Just as important is who is saying it and why, and what pressure the character is under at the time. Like Wittgenstein, we cease to listen to what is being said, and watch

153

instead the speaker's gestures. For those rants tell us more about the character than about the objective situation. Indeed, one of Bellow's points, forcibly brought out in the present novel, is that there is no 'objective situation', that the journalists — even super-journalists — and the scientists — even marvellously humane and concerned scientists — do not and cannot give it to us 'how it is', for 'it is' only how we grasp it. And this does not mean that understanding remains irremediably subjective, but that in order really to understand what is going on we must ourselves make an imaginative effort. Understanding will never simply reveal itself, it is never simply information which we can add to our existing stock; it comes only at a cost, as the result of a painful shedding of defences.

In *The Dean's December* the only things that happen are that the Dean's mother-in-law dies, and a black murderer is convicted. But what a rich book it is. Far richer, it seems to me, than the sprawling and over long *Humboldt's Gift*, which actually suffered from having too much plot. Here Albert Corde, Dean of a Chicago College and journalist, accompanies his Romanian-born wife to her country of origin to attend her mother's death. Most of the novel takes place in Bucharest in dreary mid-winter. Back home the Dean has written articles for *Harper's* blasting Chicago, and now has undertaken to fight for the conviction of two black people who killed one of the students. Obviously the Dean is not popular, either with his Provost or with the radical students, who include his nephew, a friend of the defendant. In Bucharest, with nothing to do but try to comfort his wife by his simple presence, Corde has time to ponder his life and times, helped in this by the arrival of a schoolfriend and rival, now an eminent journalist, friend and confidant of the great.

Those who know Bellow will know what to expect. I don't feel the novel breaks any new ground, except in one respect, which I shall come to in a moment. But the ground can't be gone over too often. Bellow manages to make long intellectual speeches, even internal speeches, deeply dramatic; he has an instinct for how a grey day, the bare furnishings of a room, will colour our thoughts, of the complex interconnections of daily routine and our deepest thoughts and urgings. Just as Auden made poetry capable of bearing intelligence again, so Bellow has made the novel. Yet this time round I was not entirely convinced. What had once been insights, discoveries, seem to be in danger of turning into mere tricks of style. But the problem lies deeper.

Bellow's heroes are all too aware of the temptations of imagining that horror and filth are more real than beauty and humanity. They know the romantic pull of the Chicago stockyards and their human equivalent. But Bellow himself seems to have grown curiously ambivalent. In *Humboldt's Gift* he seemed to be trying to force us to admire his realism, his deep immersion in the real — here, he was saying, was a man who hobnobbed with gangsters, who really knew what was what, not an effete ivory tower artist. But is a Chicago gangster any more real than Miss La Trobe? Part of Bellow wants to say, no, of course not, death and loss and the deep pains of the heart are the same everywhere, there are no masses, only millions of individual human beings; but part of him also wants to say: America is where it is really happening, and Chicago is where America is happening, and here am I right in the centre of it and not flinching an inch.

Contradictions don't matter if they are faced and recognised — indeed, the power of Bellow's novels up to *Herzog* lay precisely here: he sensed that only fiction could hold such contradictions together. But now I feel a lack of control, a rift right at the heart of the work. In this book, though, this is almost compensated for by one thing: Bellow has at last created a plausible and likeable woman, and he has done so with wonderful economy. Minna, the Dean's wife, is a famous astronomer, her dying mother was once Romanian Minister of Health. This sounds unlikely and unpromising, but Bellow manages to create a woman who is lovable and also — to the doting Dean — often irritating in her absorption in her stars, her failure to listen to him as he puts forward his ideas. Unlike Bellow's other women she is more than a set of theories, she is palpable in her silence and her contradictions; she and her mother and aunt make of the Romanian scenes something particularly poignant and moving.

Working so loosely, with so little plot and with the possibility of introducing almost anything, via the hero's musings, into the book, Bellow needs to have a particularly firm grasp of inner form. Here his images are never mere symbols, they are real events and objects, but they take on, even if only momentarily, the resonance of something more. They can do this for us because we sense them doing so for the hero. Here the last brief chapter recounts the trip up to the giant telescope of Mount Palomar undertaken on her return to America by the astronomer and her husband. The telescope has been booked for her, and, when they arrive, she gets into her warm suit and enters the lift. It is very very cold. The Dean accompanies her and then redescends, leaving her, small and determined, up there, to wrestle with her stars. He thinks of that other dome, in the crematorium, half way across the world, where her mother's body disappeared for ever. Momentarily he holds the two in balance. He has understood something. And so, mysteriously, have we. It is not anything that can be stated in words; it is the sum of what he and we have been living through in the course of the book. This is real art.

NOTES

**The Dean's December*, Saul Bellow, Alison Press/Secker & Warburg, 1982, £7.95

24

The Demythologising Imagination*

Günter Grass goes from strength to strength. Like his almost exact contemporary, Stockhausen, he becomes, with each new work, at once more German and more international, more personal and more universal. His last book, *The Meeting at Telgte*, was dedicated to Hans Werner Richter, the founder of Group 47, and it told of the coming together of German writers from all corners of the Empire after the devastations of the Thirty Years' War. There was no need to make explicit the parallel between 1647 and 1947; Grass let the analogy speak for itself and devoted himself to conveying the sense of a Europe exhausted and all but destroyed by war, and bringing to life a whole host of minor and largely forgotten German writers of the seventeenth century. But just because (in less than 150 pages) he succeeded so well in evoking particular artists at a particular time, the book was able to convey something about the relation of art to the realities of life at all times, everywhere. Writers, unlike businessmen and politicians, are free spirits, owing allegiance only to the truth, anxious only to emulate their great predecessors; but they are also more prone than most men to vanity, sloth, lechery and cowardice. They have very little power to change reality, and yet it is only by recognising their weaknesses and limitations that they may, perhaps, change it even if ever so slightly. Certainly if they don't no one else will.

The new book, also among the shortest he has written, is also dedicated to a writer, Nicolas Born, Grass's younger contemporary, dying of cancer as the book starts and dead by the time it finishes. It too takes as its central theme the responsibility entrusted to the writer to make holes in all the walls men build: walls round their countries, as in China; through the middle of their countries, as in Germany; round places they don't want us to examine too closely, as with nuclear installations; and around themselves. Grass has no time for those, like Rudi Dutschke, who have, as he puts it, 'a faith that refuses to be put off by reality', but it is a measure of the complexity of this short book, of its refusal to settle down comfortably in any one attitude, that Grass also gives a moving account of Dutschke's sad death, drowned in his bath during an epileptic fit brought on by the attempt on his life years earlier. But for Grass the writer's task is not to project apocalypses but to use his imagination in the service of reality; not to mythologise, as some much-praised English and American writers, drunk on the irresponsible power of the imagination, seem to think, but, on the contrary, to demythologise. What if I had been born in 1917 and not 1927? Grass asks. How would I have acted under the Nazis? What if down in South-East Asia there were only eighty million Chinese but here in the heart of Europe there were close on a billion Germans? It is the writer's function to raise these questions, to ask us to consider alternative realities, not so that we may lose ourselves in them, but so that we may recognise important facts about the reality we have: that is the product of specific choices and decisions at specific times by specific people; that we can make other choices now than the ones that appear to be forced upon us, if we so choose.

Headbirths was sparked off by a lecture tour Grass was invited to undertake in China, with Volker Schlöndorff, the maker of the film of *The Tin Drum*. In England we are used to novelists who are stuck for a subject for their next novel getting their publishers to finance a trip to some exotic region and then 'writing it up'. This form of journalism seems to be more popular with reviewers and the book-buying public than works of fiction (after all, it deals with reality, and novels are, in the end, only inventions, aren't they?), so publishers are pleased to cough up. Grass's book is not of this kind. As with Stockhausen, the very modern sense of abrupt movement from one civilisation to another has called forth from him a corresponding movement of the imagination. Back home the 1980 German elections are looming, and Grass, despite his differences with Helmut Schmidt, remains committed to the Social Democrats and their party leader Willy Brandt, and an implacable enemy of the Christian Democrats and in particular their head, Franz Josef Strauss. *Headbirths* explores the images and ideas which the simultaneous exposure to China and the German elections set off in Grass's mind.

What then is the book actually about? Well, it is about Grass and

THE DEMYTHOLOGISING IMAGINATION

Schlöndorff and their wives on the lecture tour of China; it is about a film the two men are planning, which will deal with two once-radical and now liberal schoolteachers who cannot make up their minds to have children ('Can one really bring children into the present-day world?' 'I couldn't let a child of mine be born into a Germany headed by Strauss, let's wait till after the elections...'), and who undertake a trip to India and Malaysia under the aegis of the travel firm Sisyphus, a firm which promises holidays with a difference, for with them the specially concerned can, for small extra payments, spend a night or two in the slums of Calcutta, visit refugee camps, and generally subject themselves to a sample of the miseries of the Third World; it is about Nocolas Born; about Grass himself, a novelist at the crossroads in his fifty-second year; about the two Germanies; about all German writers, past and present; about writing itself and its ambiguous relations with the powers that be.

One can imagine what the projected film, for example, might become in the hands of a Waugh or an Amis; Grass never allows himself the luxury of simple satire for the sake of laughs, nor does he imagine that he is himself so completely in possession of the truth that he can be complacent about the follies of others. He has enough in common with his two schoolteachers not to be content simply to laugh at them, ridiculous though they are — but then, Grass insists, we are all ridiculous, our only hope is to remain alive to the complexities of the world. That is really what this book is about. Grass comments disparagingly on reviewers who praised his large novels for throwing light upon the past but found no good to say about his collection of election speeches in which he tried to deal with the present and the future. Be a good boy, they seemed to be telling him, stick to the role of novelist and illuminate the past for us; as for the present, keep off it. As if in answer to this, Grass has, in his last two books, made past and present simultaneously alive, first with the single large image of the meeting at Telgte, and now with the multiple small images he calls headbirths.

A headbirth is a symbol of sterility. Perhaps it is all the Germans are good for any more. Any group that starts to worry about whether or not to have children is on its way to extinction. And this might be no bad thing, Grass suggests. After all, the Romans had their day and then disappeared. Why not the Germans? At the same time a headbirth is an imaginative projection: What if there were two ex-radical schoolteachers and they were to go off on an Asian holiday in search of reality? What if I had been born ten years earlier? What if Germany were not divided? What if we had as many Germans in the middle of Europe as there are Chinese in China? This is Kierkegaard contra Hegel. It is not the patterns of history that are important, but the moment when Cromwell or Napoleon or Abraham or you or I decide to go this way rather than that. Come with me, Grass seems to be saying, let us try this out, and then this, and then this. How does the world look to you now?

But once again the ambiguities surface. Is Grass on the defensive or the offensive? In his encounters with the Chinese he finds that he and they have unexpected ground in common. For the Chinese have just come out of their Cultural Revolution, they feel they have to learn to read and write all over again, to rediscover who and what they are after a decade of distortion and falsification. And we, says Grass, who stayed behind and lived through the Nazi years inside Germany, how can we live up to the heritage of the great *emigré* writers, Mann and Brecht? They were classics in their lifetime; we, on the other hand, can only stammer.

Note that he does not say: After Hitler only silence is possible. That too would be mythologising, giving in to the Hitler rhetoric. Stammering is the truer, more exact, more imaginative word. And Grass's books, we could say, are all stammers: false starts, hesitations, haunted by the inability to move forward, to round out the sentence, the paragraph, the work. But, like the greatest artists, he has made a strength out of weakness (Stockhausen's total eschewing of the rhythms of nineteenth-century music is no doubt connected with the association of such rhythms with the marching of jackbooted armies; yet from that rejection how much has sprung!). Grass writes: 'We've learned in school that the present comes after the past and is followed by the future. But I work with a fourth sense, the pastpresenture. That's why my form gets untidy. On my paper more is possible. Here only chaos foments order. Here even holes are contents.' In the large novels such remarks somehow convey an off-putting self-confidence; in these last two short books they are the sign of his humility, of his concern with how things *are*. He seems to have found a way of bridging the gap between a private manic inventiveness and a commitment to the complex realities of the world, between *The Tin Drum* and *From the Diary of a Snail*. Artists can't pull down the walls men build, but they can make holes in them, and if that's not much at least it's a start. In *Headbirths*, as in *The Meeting at Telgte*, Grass does not

THE DEMYTHOLOGISING IMAGINATION

merely tell us this: he shows how it can be done. It's an exhilarating performance.

NOTES

*Headbirths, or The Germans are Dying Out, Günter Grass, trans. Ralph Manheim, Secker & Warburg, 1982, £6.95

25

The Hand and the Eye*

'Le mystère Picasso' is how Clouzot entitled his famous film, in which the artist was actually seen at work before your eyes, and for most of its eight decades our century has been vainly trying to decipher that mystery. Thus to talk about Picasso is to talk about the culture of our time, not just because his work has played such an important part in it, but because in the reactions to it we can discern nearly all the myths and clichés of the age. Picasso has been the butt of every anti-modernist joke in a way Cézanne, for instance, never was, and he has also been our most celebrated artist. The paradox is only superficial, for both attitudes show little interest in the actual work of the hand or, indeed, in individual canvases.

He owed his fame to a number of factors which have little to do with art: to his longevity; to his habit of changing mistresses every ten years or so; to the fact that he was the first major artist whose rise to a position of importance coincided with a revolution in the dissemination of reproductions; above all, perhaps, to his photogenic qualities. The squat, powerful figure, feet planted firmly in the sand, bare torso gleaming, bright eyes piercing the viewer — in the last twenty years of his long life it was that image rather than any of the things he had made which immediately sprang to mind when the name Picasso was mentioned. And this is understandable. A canvas doesn't hold out much hope for you, but with Picasso around there was always the feeling that perhaps, somewhere, the secret of immortality did exist. Picasso wasn't like any of us, but we could perhaps share in his god-like status. The blurb to Donald Douglas Duncan's book of photographs — a selection from his previous books brought out, like Penrose's slightly similar *Portrait of Picasso*, to coincide with the centenary — catches the tone exactly:

Through these extraordinary photographs, reproduced in duotone and full colour, and the delightfully candid text, we can feel the vitality of this great man, watch while he creates a masterpiece, and sense the emotional depth of a genius whose work affected the entire course of modern art.

And all this for only £12.95. It's better than a holiday in Tahiti.

No wonder younger artists wanted to get him off their backs, or that discerning critics felt that Picasso the Genius was even more of a hindrance to a true appreciation of the art of our time than Picasso the Charlatan. But the curious fact is that when Michael Ayrton in the 1950s or John Berger in the 1960s tried to react to the generally unctuous tone of what passed for Picasso criticism, they produced essays which rebounded more on themselves than on Picasso, though they are surely among the finest writers on art of the past half century.

The old fox refused to be caught. Though he obviously loved to be photographed, he was not in the least concerned with his own image. Françoise Gilot said she couldn't go on living with a monument, but that may have been sour grapes. No doubt he was passionately concerned with himself, but he was even more concerned with the things he made. And not with those he *had* made, but with whatever he happened to be working on at the time. He kept the *Demoiselles d'Avignon* in his studio for twenty years, hardly ever took part in group shows when it might have advanced his career, and never evinced any desire to sell himself to the public.

In fact, he belonged more to the generation of Monet and Cézanne than to that of Pollock or Warhol. He never wrote about art, though he spoke about it without inhibition. But his comments are always reactions to immediate situations, not pondered statements or manifestos, like those of Klee or Kandinski.[1] He was perfectly happy to contradict himself, and his remarks were often trite. Yet they could also on occasion be incisive and profound, as when he said to Hélène Parmelin: 'Freedom, one must be very careful with that. In painting as in everything else. Whatever you do, you find yourself once more in chains. And there you have it, chains.' And went on to tell Jarry's story of the anarchist soldiers on parade who, told to face right, immediately all face left. Or when he answered Sabartès's query about why the sight of sea urchins interested him: 'Had I seen them only in my imagination I might not have noticed them, even if they had been in front of me. The sense of sight enjoys being surprised. If you pretend to see what is in front of you you are distracted by the idea in your mind.... It's the same law which governs humous. Only the unexpected sally makes you laugh.'

It's a pity that, with remarks like these before them, and with the mounting evidence of the painting, his staunchest supporters should have tried to account for *the* mystery of Picasso, as if that were not just one more idea in the mind. Penrose's book, first published in 1951 and now reprinted and brought up-to-date for the centenary, strikingly demonstrates the way in which even the best-intentioned critics have allowed the idea of Picasso to obscure their view of what was actually before them. Of course, as Meyer Schapiro once remarked, 'To perceive the aims of the art of one's own times and to judge them rightly is so unnatural as to constitute an act of genius',[2] but Penrose was not writing in 1914 or even 1934, but in 1951. One might have expected better.

For what we have here is part historical romance, part hagiography, strongly reminiscent of that child's life of Raphael which made such an impression on the young Sartre. Here, for example, is Penrose's description of Picasso and his father arriving in Barcelona in 1895:

> The distinguished, middle-aged man, slightly stooping, had a look of disillusionment, a sad resignation, whereas the small heir to his fading talents walked erect, alert like a young lion cub watching all round and ready to seize any objective that might be captured by his intelligence and played with, tenderly or ruthlessly, according to his mood.

Is a book which deals with biography in this way likely to illuminate the art? 'Picasso', we are told, 'is not frightened to approach the frontiers of madness, knowing that without taking this risk it is impossible to question the reality of what we see.' The present tense suggests an intimacy with the artist which the author does not hesitate to impress upon us at every opportunity. But though Picasso may have allowed Penrose to enter his house, he has certainly not succeeded in making him enter the spirit of his art. For what risk is Penrose talking about here? Is he not simply peddling the fashionable image of the Romantic artist?

For it is not just that Penrose does not write very well or think very clearly; it is that the principles of explanation on which he relies are totally at odds with what Picasso is up to. Here, for example, is his attempt to explain the distortions of the Blue Period figures:

THE HAND AND THE EYE

> In considering the act of perception, Picasso was always amazed at the discrepancy between seeing an object and knowing it. Its superficial appearance was to him absurdly inadequate. Seeing is not enough.... There are other faculties of the mind which must be brought into play if perception is to lead to an understanding. It is somewhere at the point of junction between sensual perception and the deeper regions of the mind that there is a metaphorical inner eye that sees and feels emotionally. Through this eye of the imagination it is possible to see, to understand and to love even without sight in the physical sense, and this inner seeing may be all the more intense when the windows on the outer world are closed.

This is pernicious because it gives the reader the vague sense of profundity, of true understanding, while actually blocking the way to understanding. It is just possible that Kandinsky or Gorky could be approached in this fashion, but Picasso? If ever anybody looked hard at what was in front of him it was Picasso ('The sense of sight enjoys being surprised'). But Penrose is unrelenting in his attempt to perpetuate the myth of the Romantic genius filled with an inner vision which is at odds with the world. 'He needed new and wider horizons', he tells us as he introduces the emergence of Cubism, 'and these he found not through the tiresome and confused arguments of painters, but by confidence in his own imagination, nourished by his understanding of poetry and his love of the shapes it took before his eyes.' 'Nourished by poetry' presumably seeks to elevate Picasso's imagination above the tedious banalities of mere painting. I doubt if Ponge would have thanked him for the compliment.

As often happens when something new, important, yet profoundly mysterious enters the world of art, both artists and critics hurry to defend it without really grasping its full implications, and, once a particular line of defence has been taken, it is difficult to rid oneself of it however little relation it actually bears to the facts. Thus, in the 1950s, the notion that the *nouveau roman* was *chosiste*. And thus with Cubism. Penrose writes:

> Under the rigorous dissection of analytical Cubism objects had lost their momentary superficial appearance; they had been made to reveal their existence as entities plotted in time and space. The new sense of objects conceived in three or even four dimensions seen from many angles surpassed the narrow conventions which required the single viewpoint of Vitruvian perspective.

What, one wonders, is a superficial appearance? Is it opposed to a profound appearance? And is the writer contrasting narrow conventions with broad or loose ones? Yet Douglas Cooper, in similar vein, tells us that the concern of Cubism was 'the solid, tangible reality of things', while John Golding, in a standard work on the subject, defines it as 'the fusion of various views of a figure or an object into one coherent whole', and Marshall McLuhan sums up the received opinion on the subject by saying that 'Cubism, by giving the inside and outside, the top, bottom, back and front and the rest, in two dimensions, drops the illusion of perspective in favour of an instant sensory awareness of the whole.'

What is wrong with this view is that it confuses the picture with the objects depicted in the picture, a point well made by Leo Steinberg in an essay which should finally have put paid to such notions.[3] Steinberg shows how both the purpose of Cubism and its effect on the viewer are quite other than what Penrose, Golding and McLuhan suggest:

> Cubism sought neither a three-dimensional nor a 'scientific' grasp of depicted form. Whatever objects or portions of objects remained recognisable during its 'Analytical' phase (1909-12) were not faceted to demonstrate real structures, but the better to absorb the dismembered parts in the field. In the maturity of Cubism, human figures and implements, having crystallized into angular planes, began to break up; the facets disengaged, tipped and quivered into the thickening ground. The old hollowspace of narrative painting closed in. Pictorial space became a vibrating shallow of uncertain density.

After analysing the 1910 *Girl with Mandolin*, Steinberg concludes that 'the depicted objects disintegrate beyond grasping.... The material elements of the painting become ever more palpable on the surface, the objects to which they allude ever more evanescent.'

There is no doubt that Steinberg is right. Cubism destroys the stable relation between background and foreground that had existed since the Renaissance; it does not seek to give us the object 'as it really is'. Indeed, the disintegration of the object, always stopping short of complete disappearance, is the theme and subject-matter of Cubism, and what drives Picasso forward into more and more surprising regions with a logic from which he neither can nor wants to escape. It is the great merit of Daix and Rosselet's monumental catalogue of the Cubist years that they manage to convey the sense of the possibilities facing Picasso at every stage, and thus to make us appreciate the more the choices he actually made.

Since the book appeared scholars have been sniping at the authors over matters of ascription and relative chronology. I am not competent to judge the merits of the case, but it seems to me that the 200-page introduction to the catalogue proper constitutes one of the most stimulating essays yet written about Picasso and about Cubism. The authors realise that the issues raised by Cubism include questions unthinkable to Penrose: What constitutes a work of art? Can one look at a single work and pronounce on it in isolation from the rest of the artist's output, and, if not, does this mean we have to fall back on old-fashioned biographical criticism? 'The picture hook is the ruination of painting,' Picasso was to remark much later. 'As soon as [a painting] is bought and hung on a wall ... the painting is done for.' What does this mean? One of the things it means is that the relation between artist and work, and between viewer and work, which has dominated art since the Renaissance, can no longer be taken for granted (it turns out to have been the result of the needs of a particular society). But if paintings are not to go on the walls then what are they *for*? And what is our relation to them?

The early years of the century witnessed a general crisis in western art, a more particular crisis in French art, and a specific crisis in Picasso's art. Between 1905 and 1907 he grows more and more dissatisfied with his own work, and this culminates in his blotting out of the portrait of Gertrude Stein and escaping to the Pyrenean village of Gosol. Daix and Rosselet manage to avoid seeing these years through the wrong end of the telescope — that is, backwards from the *Demoiselles d'Avignon*. They convey what it was like to grope towards that work when it was not yet in existence. Though they stress the move away from Cézanne, they rightly insist that there was not 'an isolated encounter with Cézanne, one single revelation of African art, but an interwoven series of dialogues'. And so, slowly and hesitantly, the great work came into being. But is it even finished? As with *The Waste Land* and *A la recherche*, it gives the impression of being both utterly necessary and the product of a whole series of chances, of barely recognised impulses, and of the randomness of contingent events. But perhaps these mighty works had to come out like that: once they were done one could see that that was how they had to be, but greater clarity in the process would perhaps have been too much for their makers to bear.

Already in the Gosol still-lives Picasso had been moving towards a merging of foreground and background; work on the *Demoiselles* made him grasp more clearly what it was he was after: 'By destroying the theoretical illusion of depth when he revised the *Demoiselles*, Picasso made space itself an integral part of the construction.' And yet, as the authors point out, also taking the 1910 *Girl with Mandolin* as their example, though the closed form is shattered, the presence of the woman still comes through very strongly. Indeed, what affects us is precisely the tension between presence and dispersal, as though the sense of presence grew with the possibility of dispersal and destruction — a fact seized upon with great intensity by both Virginia Woolf and Francis Bacon, and explicitly seen by Walter Benjamin as the essence of the modernist revolution, an insight which makes Benjamin, even today, modernism's most profound theorist.

Unlike Braque, Picasso always needed to violate his own too perfect finish. There was a frenzy in him to see just how far he could go in the process of disintegration without the subject's disappearing altogether. And so we move from analytic Cubism to the pasted-paper revolution and the free use of lettering. But the question is always, as it is in *Tristram Shandy*: what is the minimum requirement for the creation of conventional, illusionist space? Picasso, unlike some of his contemporaries, never used Cubism merely decoratively, but always as a tool for understanding, a 'seeing machine'.

It is the detail of *The Cubist Years* which makes it so exciting, but the grasp of detail depends on an awareness of what the larger issues are. What Daix and Rosselet have to say about the period 1907-16 illuminates the entire *oeuvre*, for their fundamental principle is this: Picasso gave painting back a renewed sense of its possibilities, and he did this not just through a succession of amazing masterpieces, but through the totality of his creative life. Mistakes, blind alleys — these are as important as the successes. Look at any spot in the Cubist years and you see only failure, destruction; look at the whole period and what you see is a miracle of invention and reconstruction.

Frank Russell's study of *Guernica* to some extent bears out this contention. We know so much about the background to the painting and the stages it went through that it was a good idea to study it in detail and in the way he does. I have never seen an art book designed quite like this one. Often there are as many as five or six fragments of the painting on the page, punctuating the text rather like the Chinese ideograms in the *Cantos*, reinforcing the argument as a lecturer would do by pointing to the relevant detail on the screen. Russell takes the work to pieces, treating it rather like a poem which is made up of innumerable individual words and phrases. And the publishers have done him proud. At the end of the book we may have been taken over the same square foot of canvas fifteen or twenty times, as Russell examines it from different points of view. In the process a great deal about that disturbing painting is brought to light, not least Picasso's persistent drive towards simplification and clarification, his desire to eschew easy emotionalism and the kind of political gesture which is often taken as 'serious' because it shouts very loudly that the baddies are bad and the victims innocent. Russell shows how the image of the bull, for example, which Picasso could so easily have made into the symbol of evil, and which does indeed undergo an almost continuous metamorphosis in the course of the composition, eventually emerges as more baffled and helpless than ferocious, and how the classic nature of the composition reinforces this refusal to pass judgement.

Ultimately, though, I felt that there was an element of overkill in Russell's book. What might have been fascinating as a series of lectures tended to become slightly tedious as the ground was gone over yet again from a new perspective. Nevertheless, it is a balanced and careful study of one of the greatest paintings of the century, and should suffice to put paid to the arguments of those purists who insist that Picasso did nothing good after his Cubist years.

Guernica, with its innumerable preliminary sketches and echoes in earlier minotaur paintings, raises in different fashion the questions already posed by Daix and Rosselet. Though here we can still talk of sketches *for* a major composition, it is already becoming clear that there was a deep impulse at work in Picasso to create art in terms of series, of variations on a theme, rather than in terms of major single compositions. This impulse had obviously always been there, but it was only in his later years that he became fully conscious of it and quite deliberately worked with rather than against it.

The need to work with variation form stems from the artist's sense that the world will reveal itself not through the one transcendental illumination but through the interplay of constant approximations. It thus fits in with Picasso's humility and his insatiable desire for work, but we must try to realise how very much it went against the grain of artistic endeavour as it had been codified in the West since the Renaissance. Yet Picasso was not alone in this. Stravinsky too, from *Petrushka* on, developed a style based on repetition and variation, and

Wallace Stevens quite consciously developed variation rather than sonata form, as Hockney sensed when he decided to make his own variations on Stevens's variations on Picasso's *Man with the Blue Guitar*.

The *Las Meninas* series and especially the late erotic series known as *Suite 347* (347 etchings executed at Mougins in eight months in 1968) seem to me to be among Picasso's most profound and moving works. In the latter, at long last, form and content, theme and approach, play with and against each other in an extraordinary demonstration of the interconnection of wit and despair. Here Picasso explores at length what had always been his central insight: the irresolvable paradox of creation. At its simplest — and we are, in these late etchings, for all their flourishes, as much at the bedrock of art as we are in *The Winter's Tale* and *The Tempest* — at its simplest, to paint is: not to live. In Picasso's shorthand this means: not to make love. But to make nothing but love is to sink into boredom, cynicism and despair. To paint, on the other hand, is to come alive to a world of infinite possibility. Picasso does not make us aware of this as, say, Morandi does, by the patient exploration of that which is there, but rather by the feverish yet witty exploration of the inevitable shortcomings of art. The ultimate shortcoming is that it seems to introduce us to a world free of time, yet the making of this world takes up time.

Time weighs heavily on Picasso, as it does on all Spanish artists. His sense of time passing is not the result of his great age, it had been there from the start, as simply one aspect of the world into which we are all born. But age certainly sharpened the feeling, as it did for Stevens. Yet if time is ultimately destructive, it is also ultimately beneficial, for it is time that allows the hand to move across the canvas, and to move again and erase or alter what has been done. Picasso's insistence on process, his refusal of the notion of masterpiece, stems from his insight that to deny time is to deny that which makes one most essentially human. And in the end it is his humanity which is the most striking thing about him. I am not talking of humanity with a capital H, but of what it means to be a human being, of *everything* it means to be a human being.

This was strikingly borne out by the last surprise Picasso had in store for us, the revelation of those works he had kept for himself and which he left to the French government in lieu of death duties. Before being permanently housed in a Picasso museum in Paris they were exhibited at the Grand Palais, then in the Museum of Modern Art in New York, and at the Hayward Gallery, London. Ideally they should be seen along with the works by other artists which Picasso collected in the course of his life and which are now on permanent display at the Louvre. And Thames & Hudson, in conjunction with the New York Museum of Modern Art, have brought out a splendid volume which is the catalogue of the show, called *Pablo Picasso, A Retrospective*. That, however, is no substitute for an actual visit.

As I walked round the Grand Palais last year I was filled with a sense of sheer joy which I had not experienced for a long time. Every item in the exhibition, from the tiniest matchstick construction to the largest oil, gave one the sense of absolute rightness, of perfect realisation. Curiously, I had just been attending the splendid series of concerts given by the London Sinfonietta and the London Symphony Orchestra to commemorate Stravinsky, and there too I had sensed just this kind of clarity, wit and humanity in even the tiniest work. What Stravinsky and Picasso had in common was a sense of the way an idea could be realised with the minimum of fuss, and the ability to see the skeleton of the form as an integral part of the meaning without ever descending into mere formalism. And what they both had was that special brand of humanism which consists in seeing man realistically as only one part of the universe — but which, seeing him thus, gives him back his sense of potential. I realised too how many of the paintings and even sculptures dealt with two figures, and of the tenderness of their relations to each other. Hockney, in a recent radio conversation with Edward Lucie-Smith, drew attention to the marvellous painting of the mother teaching her child to walk. In the distortions of the mother's face one sees all the anxiety and love a mother has for her child as he begins, quite literally, to move away from her; in the equally distorted face of the child we see a different kind of anxiety: will he make it? will he fall? — along with a kind of stubborn pride and determination: Yes, he will make it — the great human adventure is beginning once again. A universal subject, said Hockney, but how many painters apart from Picasso have tackled it? And he didn't add what is perhaps the most surprising thing about this tender, domestic work: that it was done in 1943, in the middle of the war.

The 'mystère Picasso' is not a mystery forever removed from us, nor one to which we simply need the key in order to unlock it. It is there in the works; we need only open ourselves to them and explore. We will never pluck out the heart of the mystery not because it has no heart or that heart is perpetually hidden, but because the heart lies in the movement — the movement of the hand in each canvas and construction, the movement from work to work. Picasso gives us back nothing less than our possible world: what is always possible for each one of us, but which the deadening hand of habit keeps making us forget.

NOTES

*Pablo Picasso: A Retrospective, ed. William Rubin, Thames & Hudson, for the Museum of Modern Art, New York, 1980

Picasso: His Life and Work, Roland Penrose, enlarged reprint, Granada, 1981

Portrait of Picasso, Roland Penrose, enlarged edition, Thames & Hudson, 1981

Viva Picasso: A Centennial Celebration, 1881-1981, Donald Douglas Duncan, Allen Lane, 1981

Picasso: The Cubist Years, 1907-1916, Pierre Daix and Joan Rosselet, Thames & Hudson, 1980

Picasso's Guernica: The Labyrinth of Vision, Frank D. Russell, Thames & Hudson, 1980

1 Many of his remarks have been collected by Dore Ashton in *Picasso on Art: A Selection of Views*, London, 1972. But they seem false when taken out of context, and are no substitute for books like Brassai's *Picasso & Company*, however doubtful one feels about its complete authenticity.
2 Introduction to Eugène Fromentin's *The Old Masters of Belgium and Holland*, New York, 1963. Schapiro's modest little essay on Picasso's *Woman with a Fan*, reprinted in the second volume of his selected papers, *Modern Art*, London, 1978, is probably the best short piece on Picasso.
3 'The Algerian Women and Picasso at Large', in *Other Criteria: Confrontations with Twentieth Century Art*, New York, 1972. Part of this essay is reprinted in the useful volume, *Picasso in Perspective*, ed. Gert Schiff, New Jersey, 1976.

26
Conclusion: From the Other Side of the Fence, or True Confessions of an Experimentalist

It is a shock to any artist who has only thought of getting things 'right', of pinning down that elusive feeling which is the source and end of all creative activity, to wake up one morning and find himself labelled 'experimental'. Yet that is what happened to me. When my novel *Migrations* was published in 1977 *The Times* fiction reviewer, Susan Hill, wrote: 'I find it impossible to assess Giles Gordon's *Enemies* and Gabriel Josipovici's *Migrations* with any confidence, because I found them hard to read, belonging as they both do to a sub-branch of contemporary fiction with which I have never been greatly in sympathy.' However, she went on kindly, 'Josipovici's ... example of the genre ... will add considerably to his hard-earned reputation as an experimental novelist.' I was still puzzling over that 'hard-earned' (did she really think writing novels was that kind of hard work, or was she making some more subtle and insulting suggestion?), when I opened the *Daily Telegraph* and read: 'Mr. Josipovici may be trying to create a literary equivalent of abstract painting.... Or he may be seeking an equivalent for music.... But don't let me put you off: Britain is short enough of experimental writers without my dissuading readers from the few there are.'

Four years and two novels later the majority of reviewers were still reiterating the same views: 'Josipovici's preoccupation with expanding the possibilities of the novel is leading him towards a formal and stylistic sophistication operating in a vacuum', opined the *Times Literary Supplement*; while Graham Hough, in the *London Review of Books*, suggested that I was 'prominent among those who are anxious to free the novel from any hampering subservience to the outer world', but also that I tried deliberately to make things difficult for the reader either out of a perverse desire to mystify or (reviewers like to hedge their bets) 'to enrich the reader's apprehension', and darkly warned that we had here 'a lingering but still severe case of the Robbe-Grillet syndrome'.

All these, and most other reviews I received for those two novels, *Migrations* and *The Air We Breathe*, seemed to share the same assumptions: there are writers and there are experimental writers; the 'experimental' is a sub-branch of fiction, rather like teenage romances or science fiction perhaps, but differing from them in being specifically highbrow, and, like other highbrow activities, such as abstract painting and classical music, it is totally unconnected with the real world; however, we should tolerate this for the health of art (and to show how tolerant we are).

This is surely a farrago of nonsense. None of these critics has really thought through what it would mean for any art 'to be freed from subservience to the outer world', or why any artist would be interested in doing this, or in 'expanding the possibilities of the medium'. I think we can leave music and painting to fight their own battles. Few people are still outraged by *Les Demoiselles d'Avignon* or *Le Sacre du printemps*, though naturally their contemporary equivalents are still greeted with indignation. The difference is that, by and large, art and music critics see their function as that of middlemen, helping viewers and listeners to come to terms with the most interesting aspects of modern art, while fiction reviewers still see themselves as somehow the guardians of the point of view of the man in the street.

The interesting question is why a reviewer should speak quite naturally of 'a lingering but still severe case of the Robbe-Grillet syndrome' but never, in the case of most novels being produced today, of 'a severe case of the Charlotte Brontë or the George Eliot syndrome'? Why is there this presumption that the novel as written by these two writers is somehow *natural*, while that written by Robbe-Grillet (here used rather as the name Picasso used to be, as synonymous with 'meaningless and insulting avant-garde rubbish', regardless of whether the work in question has any real resemblance to either artist) — while that written by Robbe-Grillet is fabricated-with-intent-to-be-clever, or even with-intent-to-deceive-and-confuse?

What I found most puzzling about the reviewers' response to my two novels was that not only was I convinced that they were the best of the six novels I had written, but both were written more directly from the heart than anything else of mine. If I had any doubts about them it was that they were too raw, too personal. Yet here I was being told they were too 'abstract', too interested in form for its own sake (the generous reviews), too concerned merely to make things difficult out of a desire to shock or earn myself a reputation as an avant-garde writer (the most hostile ones). Clearly there was a failure of communication somewhere. Though there was no sex or violence in either novel, they had obviously upset the reviewers. (Was it perhaps just *because* there was no sex or violence in them? One never knows these days.) Trying to interpret their own feelings of frustration and annoyance, the reviewers had reached for the first word that came to hand: the novels were 'experimental'. Now they could relax; they knew where they were, and they could either castigate me for insulting my public, or praise me for doing an unremunerative but necessary job (every advanced nation has to have its experimental writers) as well as I could be expected to, in the circumstances.

One could say that experimental theatre is the kind of group improvisatory theatre that works without scripts. There are of course good and bad plays produced in this way, but the distinction between 'experimental' and 'traditional' can be made in the theatre: experimental theatre works without scripts; traditional theatre works with them. The distinction, however, cannot in the nature of things apply to fiction. Moreover, no novelist ever sits down at his desk and writes his books straight off, never revising, never scratching out, never trying another angle or scrapping what he has done and starting again. It seems as if writers like Nashe and Sterne and Beckett are exceptions to this rule, but scholars are quick to point out that the apparently impromptu nature of their work is a rhetorical strategy, that the pretence of offhandedness is itself a highly conscious device. I am not sure. I suspect that there *is* an element of the impromptu in these writers. Beckett, especially in *The Unnamable*, does seem to move forward in an extraordinarily unpremeditated way, as though the thing had come in one great burst and it was all he could do to get it down. The traditional novelist, on the other hand, is known to write slowly, revising as he goes, deliberating at each sentence about how he will go on, sometimes pausing for hours to select the right word. So perhaps we should really call George Eliot or Henry James or Barbara Pym experimental, and Sterne and Beckett natural.

But this wouldn't be quite right either. Shakespeare and Mozart are supposed never to have blotted a line or revised their work; but all this means is that the process of selection and revision went on in their heads as they were working; they simply thought faster and to better effect than others. Beckett may now have written many drafts of *The Unnamable*, but all he had written up to that time could be considered as drafts. Art is never spontaneous, natural, it is always a matter of what Gombrich has called matching and making; it is simply that criticism is too clumsy to grasp the creative process.

What we have then is not so much a stark opposition between the traditional and the experimental, as a kind of spectrum, with, in this century Graham Greene, say, at one end, and Joyce at the other. It is easy to see that *Ulysses* (and even more *Finnegans Wake*) is a totally different kind of thing from *The Heart of the Matter*. Its aims are different, its mode of construction is different, the claims it makes on its readers are different. But if we fill in the spectrum thus: Greene-Waugh-Spark-Golding-Woolf-Beckett-Joyce, then the problem becomes acute somewhere in the middle. Does the line of demarcation come between Waugh and Spark? Or between Spark and Golding? Or between Golding and Woolf? Or between Woolf and Beckett? Don't we feel that what distinguishes *all* these writers, what makes them among the best we have had in this century, is precisely the sense all of them convey (my only doubts concern Graham Greene) of having got it absolutely right for themselves — for what they wanted to say? They have felt so strongly about what they wanted to say that they have not rested till they have found precisely how it could best be conveyed.

What does 'getting it right' mean for the novelist? Perhaps I can give an example from the work I know best, my own. When I wrote my first novel, *The Inventory* (1968), I did not know if I would be able to do what I had always dreamt of doing one day, write a novel. At that point there were many overlapping pressures which ensured that the book got written, and that it was this particular book and not another. But I had terrible problems with the opening. I knew how I wanted to start: a solicitor arrives at a house to take an inventory of the belongings of a dead man. I knew I had to start with the solicitor arriving at this house. I could visualise the house and in what part of London it stood. But every time I tried to write the scene I found it collapsing under me. Should I describe the house in one paragraph? In two? In a page? A sentence? This seems a trivial difficulty, and indeed I had not given it a thought when I was coming to grips with the theme and shape of the book. But as I struggled with it I realised

CONCLUSION

more and more clearly that whatever I was wanting to do it was not what I was doing. And yet in the end was I not writing only because I wanted to? So what was wrong?

I knew the book had to start with this particular scene. (In the end, as it happens, it didn't; that scene came third.) Why couldn't I get it written? I found myself trying to write it by adopting an ironical tone, a whimsical tone, a reportorial tone — none of it was right. I simply couldn't find the descriptive tone I wanted. I was mimicking the tones of every novel I had ever read, and I wasn't happy with any of them. But then what did I want? What was I after?

Suddenly it came to me: it was not just the tone that was wrong; it was the whole approach. I was adopting, unthinkingly, not just the tone of every novel I had ever read, but also the assumptions. First and foremost among these was the assumption that if someone, in a novel, arrives at a house or enters a room for the first time, that house or room must be described. But was this an absolute law of narrative? I suddenly realised that it was nothing of the sort. It was a convention. And, because it was only a convention, I suddenly saw that I could do without it. I could actually get on with what really interested me, which was the introduction of the solicitor to the surviving family of the deceased, gathered in the house, without having to describe the house at all. I simply had to start the different characters talking, thus:

'Mr Stout? said the woman who opened the door.

'Hyman,' said Joe. 'Mr. Stout's on holiday. In Corsica.'

'Gill said it would be Mr. Stout,' said the woman doubtfully.

Joe shrugged.

'They could at least have sent one of their permanent staff,' said the woman.

'I am one of their permanent staff,' said Joe.

'You look like a student,' said the woman.

'As a matter of fact,' said Joe, 'and if you want to be quite precise, I *am* their permanent staff.'

'You'd better come in,' said the woman.

'Thank you,' said Joe.

'I'll lead,' said the woman. 'Close the door behind you and give it a push or it won't stay shut.'

'I'm afraid,' he said to the woman, 'I stepped on something which gave a kind of squeak.'

'What kind of squeak?'

'Well ... sort of high-pitched, I suppose.'
'Don't worry,' she said. 'That was probably one of Mick's toys. He leaves them about everywhere. I hope you broke it.'
'I rather think I felt it move,' he said.
'Some of them even do that,' she said. 'But it may have been Oscar.'
'It felt more like Oscar,' he confessed.

Years later I came across a remark by Stravinsky in one of his conversations with Robert Craft. He was talking about the discovery, early on in his career, that 'one important characteristic of Russian popular verse is that the accents of the spoken verse are ignored when the verse is sung'. And he commented: 'The recognition of the musical possibilities inherent in this fact was one of the most rejoicing discoveries of my life. I was like a man who suddenly finds that his finger can be bent from the second joint as well as from the first.' Discovering that I could do it all in dialogue in that first novel was rather like that for me.

The point I am trying to make is that the distinction is not between 'experimental' and 'non-experimental' art, but between successful and unsuccessful solutions to problems. I suppose there is no such thing, strictly speaking, as an unsuccessful solution. If the artist is aware of something that *needs* a solution, he will find it. Looking at the history of art one sees that for most of the time artists aren't even aware that there is a problem. And the difference is really between the writer who, whether by instinct or by thought, 'gets it right', and the one who imagines he is writing what he feels, what he wants, but who is really only reproducing someone else's way of feeling. All talk of plagiarism pales before this much deeper and more prevalent kind of unacknowledged borrowing, which is the mode of working of nine artists out of ten.

But how then can one decide when a writer has 'got it right' for himself and when he hasn't? The answer is, by using one's ear. But this is hardly an answer at all. The question really is: how does one tell the good writer from the bad? And this is actually a very odd question indeed. It is probably only one that could be asked in an age like ours, where we ask both too many and too few questions of art. Today it seems to be becoming harder and harder for us to remember that books are not objects to be evaluated or items of entertainment, but friends to be listened to.

CONCLUSION

Of course we read books to get through exams, or to get through uncomfortable railway journeys, or when we are too tired to do anything else. But that does not exhaust the value of books, that is not why books have been preserved by men for three thousand years. It is because they give us something which only our closest friends can give us, yet we can choose any of them we like and meet them when and how we like. That is the miracle of books.

We don't judge our friends and we cannot justify them. We never ask: What do they mean? We only know that there are some people we want to see more of, and others we want to avoid. I do not like the novels of Virginia Woolf more than those of Kingsley Amis because I like 'experiment' better than 'tradition', but because I would rather spend a few hours in her company than in his. And that does not mean reading her letters or a biography of her, interesting as these may be. She herself felt that she was most herself in her novels, and it is there I like to meet her. Would I say then that Virginia Woolf was a better writer than Amis? I want to say yes, but in order to defend that judgement I would have to lay bare such deep layers of myself that I wonder if it's worth it. We don't try to explain why we want to see a certain person again or avoid another. We just do it. And even if I were to try to defend my judgement I would almost certainly not be able to persuade someone who held a contrary view. Does this mean that literary judgements are hopelessly subjective? I don't think so, because with literature as distinct from people we find ourselves moving on, we find we have a growing awareness of what is good and what is bad, and we discover that books never let us down: we may outgrow some of them or grow into an appreciation of others, but that is all.

And we don't always like people for the same reason. One has many different friends, whom one likes to see for different reasons at different times. Bernard Malamud's *Dubin's Lives*, Georges Perec's *La Vie mode d'emploi*, and Rosalind Belben's *Dreaming of Dead People* could not be more different from each other, yet they are all recognisably novels, and they are all masterpieces. With the first the fiction reviewers of *The Times* and the *Daily Telegraph* would presumably have no difficulty (though they are unlikely to have fathomed its depths at a first reading). The second runs to 700 pages, is made up of ninety-nine chapters, is based on complex permutational laws, is one of the funniest books I have ever read, won the Prix Femina in France, and has passed totally unnoticed in this country. Perec died tragically at the age of forty-six; I cannot see any of his books being translated into

English in the immediate future, unless publishers and the Arts Council suddenly become much more imaginative than they are at present; yet to my mind *La vie mode d'emploi* is an even better novel than *Ulysses*. Rosalind Belben's book is more meditation than narrative and incorporates a number of medieval lyrics; yet it is as much a novel as *A la recherche du temps perdu* and *To the Lighthouse*. It was well received when it came out in 1979, yet somehow has failed to establish itself as the major work it undoubtedly is. All three are among the half dozen novels that have meant most to me in the last decade. I know I shall go on re-reading them — they are friends for life. When I come across crass reviews or throw away much-touted novels after three or four pages, I remind myself that with three such novels published in the last five years the state of fiction today can only be regarded as pretty healthy. My advice to anyone who asks about 'experimental' writing today would be: forget about labels and go out and buy these three books. Reviewers may be influential, but in the end it's the writers who count. And the good writers will go on producing the books they have to regardless of the reviewers.

Acknowledgements

I should like to thank the editors of the following journals, in which these reviews first appeared, for giving me the chance to write them, and for permission to reprint them here:

Books and Bookmen for 'From the Other Side of the Fence, or True Confessions of an Experimentalist'.

The Jewish Quarterly for 'A Ghost in the City'.

The Listener for 'Life and Letters'; 'Saneness and Wisdom'; 'A Childish Vision'; 'The Ethics of Silence'; 'A Modern Poet'; 'On the Brink of Parable'.

The London Review of Books for 'True Mastery'; 'Reading the Middle Ages'; 'A Great Critic'; 'A Life and a Half'; 'Three Thousand Years of Poetry'; 'Radiance and Interpretation'; 'The Hand and the Eye'.

The New York Review of Books for 'What Was Chaucer Really Up To?'; 'Rabelais and the Role of Fiction'.

Quarto for 'A Sense of Waste'; 'The Heart of the Matter'.

The Sunday Times for 'A Happy Man'; 'The Last Great Book'.

The Times Literary Supplement for 'A Triumphant Return'; 'The Really Real'; 'The Demythologising Imagination'.